Visiting Hours
Are Over

A Chaplain Discovers
What Really Matters
From Her Parents' Deaths

Janna Flynn Roche

Dedication

*This book is dedicated to Bell-Jo Rodgers
whose lifelong commitment to improving the time
of those who are dying has had incredible impact not
only on countless individual lives but also on the
Williamsburg community.*

CONTENTS

Author and her siblings in order of birth.

Sister	Profession	Home State
Linnea	*Professor of Psychiatric Nursing*	*IL*
Janna (author)	*Health Care Chaplain*	*VA*
Marilee	*Artist and Frame Shop Owner*	*FL*
Annilee	*Lawyer (retired)*	*MD*
Donna	*Database Analyst*	*NY*
Carol	*Teacher*	*SD*
Susan	*Telecommunications Engineer*	*MD*

Janna Flynn Roche

Prelude

When I was still in my twenties, I went on a visit to my childhood home. Without much preamble, my mother decided to educate me as to what I'd need to know if something happened to her or to my father. I dimly recall our tour around the house. She led me to closets and drawers where jewelry and significant papers were stored. Primarily my memory is of a clanging in my head that prevented me from comprehending the words she was speaking. Apparently the thought that my parents would die someday was not something I was able to absorb at that point in my life.

Three decades later, on another visit to my parents, I realized there had been no family discussions regarding my parents' wishes; in the event either of them became seriously ill or died. So, during this visit I tried to initiate a dialogue. However, my parents - then in their eighties – chose not to be engaged in a conversation about end-of-life decision making.

Though I felt better for attempting that difficult conversation, I was disappointed it didn't take place. Having conversations about life and death choices with anyone, when one is actually confronting the situation, is much more stressful than having them before they're necessary; and they are even more anguishing with loved ones. That's why it is so important to tackle issues of what defines a life with quality while individuals are in good health.

In those intervening decades, thanks to an incredibly supportive husband, I earned a seminary degree, became a healthcare chaplain and vigiled many hours by bedsides with individuals and families; listening to stories, laughing, weeping and praying. While working in hospices, hospitals and a retirement community, I witnessed a diversity of ending-life scenarios; some I would hope to emulate, and others I would avoid at all costs.

The primary focus of my chaplain ministry had always revolved around death. I served two Hospice organizations, and worked as a college chaplain officiating at numerous student and college memorial services. In my current arena - the retirement community - companioning individuals in their final days, providing grief support to widows and groups, and crafting and officiating at frequent memorial services compose my primary duties. I believe that it is a disservice to neglect to commemorate, in a dignified and fitting way, the life of a person when they die. The disservice is to the surviving loved ones, those who have to continue their lives in the absence of the one who has died.

Ministering in life and death encounters with my patients taught me how critical it is to share one's final wishes with family members. I would not be writing this book if our family had a serious conversation and my parents fleshed out what constituted a life of quality.

* * *

In the early 1970's, the lifespan for males was 68 and for females 75. Most deaths came relatively quickly and resulted from heart attacks, strokes, accidents or disease processes that weren't drawn out by medical or surgical intervention.

During the first half of the twentieth century, options regarding extending one's life were relatively nonexistent. Preplanning, therefore, was not imperative because the life-sustaining technologies we have now, were unavailable. Even CPR (cardiopulmonary resuscitation) was not invented until the 1960's and initially only utilized for those likely to recover. Antibiotics arrived after World War I. Thus dying, prior to relatively recent medical advancements, was more straightforward, and in most cases considered to be nature taking its course.

However, because we live in a more technologically savvy world, there is a new landscape of dying. Physicians have come to consider death more of a medical failure than a natural conclusion of life. Individuals frequently have a say in its timing and not opting for treatment has become the exception to the rule, often causing patients and family members to feel they are complicit in the death. On the other hand, opting for life-prolonging treatment, even when it is futile and causes additional suffering, is translated as caring for one's loved one or one's self as all should.

We are amid a generation of baby boomers who are companioning their parents during these last years of life and who, as a result of the unsettling experiences they're seeing, are questioning current practices and perspectives. I am one of those baby boomers that witnessed many individuals, including my parents, in their last days, and because of what I have learned, feel the need to empower others to prepare for possible worst-case scenarios, so that there's a greater likelihood suffering can be mitigated and individual wishes can be honored, whatever they may be. Based on the experiences my six sisters and I shared during my parents' dying times, my hope is that readers will glean some understanding that proves useful in the final journeys they and their loved ones eventually take.

* * *

This is a book chronicling the events leading up to and surrounding my parents' deaths. My father died in 2006, and my mother, eight years later, in 2014. The experience of their final days differed considerably, in large part due to my mother resolving, after observing the tragic circumstances my dad endured during his final months, to disallow a similar drawn-out ending for herself.

The moral of this story is that each of us is free to choose as we wish, and those who consider ahead of time what constitutes a life with quality, will have a better likelihood of realizing their wishes. It is my hope in writing this book that before you, or your loved one's visiting hours are over, you thoughtfully assess what makes life worth living, so you have a greater possibility of living with quality until you breathe your last breath.

Janna Flynn Roche

Obituary of My Father

The Reverend Leslie B. Flynn, pastor, author, teacher, radio broadcaster, husband, father, grandfather, and great-grandfather, died at home in Nanuet, New York on August 11, 2006, at age 87. Reverend Flynn was the pastor of the Grace Baptist Church in Nanuet, New York for 40 years, from 1949 until he retired in 1989, and he had been Pastor Emeritus there from 1989 until his death.

At the age of 15, Leslie Flynn claimed Psalm 37:4 as his life verse: "Delight thyself also in the Lord and he shall give thee the desires of thine heart." Reverend Flynn often said that this verse proved to be true in his life. He dedicated himself to trying to answer God's call for his life and in return he felt blessed beyond measure. Reverend Flynn enjoyed a rewarding career doing meaningful work that he loved, an active retirement, and a rich family life. Married for 61 years, he and his wife raised 7 daughters. Upon his retirement from Grace Baptist Church at the age of 70, he invoked Psalm 23:6, saying "Surely goodness and mercy have followed me all the days of my life."

Born in Hamilton, Ontario, Canada on October 3, 1918, Reverend Flynn graduated from high school at the age of 16. He completed the pastor's course at Moody Bible Institute and earned a Bachelor of Arts degree from Wheaton College, a Bachelor of Divinity degree from Eastern Baptist Seminary, and a Master of Arts degree in philosophy from the University of Pennsylvania. He was also granted an honorary Doctor of Divinity degree from Denver Seminary. Before coming to Nanuet, he was the pastor of Bethlehem Baptist Church in St. Clair, Pennsylvania from 1944 – 1949.

During his 40-year pastorate at Grace Baptist Church in Nanuet, Reverend Flynn was dedicated to his parishioners. He started each workday praying for members of his congregation individually by name. He was faithful in his visitation, making approximately 1,000 calls a year to homes and hospitals. Under his leadership, two new buildings were erected to accommodate the needs of the growing congregation. When asked how he survived 40 years in the same church, he answered, "Ultimately, through the goodness of God and the support of a kind congregation."

Reverend Flynn's ministry was not confined to his church. A prolific writer, he authored 43 books and hundreds of articles for religious magazines. His most recent book, <u>Laugh</u>, which he completed at age 87, is scheduled for publication later this year. His most popular book, <u>19 Gifts of the Spirit</u>, sold over 250,000 copies since its publication in 1973. His most widely published tract, <u>Through the Bible in a Year</u>, has had more than a million copies printed.

In addition to pastoring and writing, Reverend Flynn taught pastoral methods, journalism, and evangelism at Nyack College for 21 years. He also had weekly broadcasts on three local New York radio stations for 24 years. In addition, he filled an average of 40 speaking engagements outside the church each year. Reverend Flynn was a member of the Board of Trustees of Denver Seminary for 15 years and a member of the Board of Directors of the World Relief Commission for 20 years. Through the generosity of his church and in his capacity as a World Relief board member, he traveled extensively, visiting mission fields worldwide.

Through his ministry at the church, on the radio, in writing and in person, Reverend Flynn touched countless lives and worked tirelessly to spread God's message of love and forgiveness to all people. He was gentle, hard working, humble, disciplined, and soft-spoken. He had both an encyclopedic knowledge of the Bible and a winning sense of humor. Nothing made him happier than to see someone's life change for the better through Christ's teachings. When asked how he would like to be *remembered, he answered, "Simply, that I preached the word of God."*

Reverend Flynn is survived by his wife, Bernice Carlson Flynn; 7 daughters, Linnea Carlson-Sabelli, of Chicago, Illinois, Rev. Janna Roche of Williamsburg, Virginia, Marilee Lee of Jensen Beach, Florida, Annilee Oppenheimer of Potomac, Maryland, Donna McGrath of Ravena, New York, Carol Mellema of Sioux Falls, South Dakota, and Susan Symington of Bethesda, Maryland; 22 grandchildren; and 5 great-grandchildren. A memorial service will be held at the Grace Baptist Church in Nanuet on August 19th at 1:00 p.m.

Janna Flynn Roche

Obituary of My Mother

Bernice Carlson Flynn, 91, died of congestive heart failure on March 11, 2014 at Westminster Canterbury, a continuing care facility in Richmond, Virginia.

Born on Halloween in 1922 to Swedish and Finnish immigrant parents, Bernice grew up in Wheaton, Illinois. Her formative years were dominated by a sense of joyfulness and optimism imparted by her gregarious, entrepreneurial father. Her more retiring mother embodied the values of thrift and hard work that helped bring the dreams of Bernice's father to fruition. Bernice internalized the best qualities of both of her parents and they have served her well throughout her life.

Bernice received a B.A. in Speech from Wheaton College in 1945, and she married Leslie Bruce Flynn, a Baptist minister, later that year. They were married 61 years, until his death in 2006. They raised 7 daughters, and had 23 grandchildren and 9 great-grandchildren. Bernice served as pastor's wife for 4 years in St. Clair, Pennsylvania and then for 40 years in Nanuet, New York. After her husband's retirement from the ministry in 1989, Bernice remained in Nanuet. In 2012 she moved to Westminster Canterbury because she could no longer live independently in her home. Although Bernice was 89 and her health had begun to fail when she moved, she nevertheless vowed to "enjoy as much as I can as long as I can" and she continued to embrace life until the end.

In addition to her roles as family matriarch and pastor's wife, Bernice has been a radio program producer, family editor of Christian Life magazine, co-author of 3 books with her husband, co-owner of a nursery school, a speech teacher, a special education teacher, and an inspirational speaker at retreats and workshops. She has also traveled worldwide, both for personal pleasure and in her capacity as a member of the Board of Directors for the Conservative Baptist Foreign Mission Society.

One of Bernice's great gifts was the ability to provide encouragement to others, and her positive approach to life was contagious. Bernice believed that "there is gold within everyone" and she was able to motivate others to be their best selves.

Donations in Bernice's memory may be made to Westminster Canterbury Foundation in Richmond, Virginia.

Bernice's community at Westminster Canterbury held a memorial service for her in Richmond on March 24, 2014. In addition, Bernice's family will hold a private graveside service for her in Nanuet later this year.

Visiting Hours Are Over

Janna Flynn Roche

PART I

My Father's Story

Janna Flynn Roche

Diagnosis and Hospitalization

Several days after Christmas in 2005, my husband and I flew home to Virginia after celebrating the holiday with our son in Las Vegas. As the plane landed my cell phone indicated a voice message. At the time, I was serving as chaplain in a retirement community and I assumed I was receiving news about a resident who required immediate attention. I was mistaken. The voice mail, from my sister, was: *"Daddy has been admitted to the hospital."*

I knew my dad had not been feeling up to par for several weeks but I was surprised to hear whatever was wrong was serious enough to hospitalize him.

On Christmas day, my father had little appetite. During the next two days, while waiting for his doctor to see him, he completed the manuscript for a book he was writing (his 43rd) and sent it to the publisher. A day later, December 29th, he was transported from the doctor's office directly to the hospital.

At the time my father was eighty-seven years old. Until his retirement, seventeen years previously, he had enjoyed excellent health with no major hospitalizations. He came from hearty stock – his parents lived independently until their deaths, at ages eighty-nine and ninety, dying within a month of each other - one of pneumonia and the other from a stroke. Both experienced what is now termed, "compressed morbidity", meaning their dying times were not drawn out.

Maximizing his health legacy, even before the fitness craze, my dad maintained a disciplined lifestyle; faithfully performing Air Force exercises, walking to work, abstaining from alcohol and drugs, and maintaining his diet, although the one area where his incredible willpower was somewhat relaxed...sweets.

Before he retired at age seventy, my father served for forty years as senior pastor at a church in the suburbs of New York City. Along with all of the customary duties associated with congregational ministry - overseeing his staff, preparing two sermons weekly, tending to the ill and dying - my dad taught courses at a local seminary, had a weekly radio show and was a prolific writer.

Added to these incredibly demanding professional tasks were responsibilities on the home front. Between 1947 and 1963 he and my mother became parents of eight daughters. (Sadly their eighth daughter died the day she was born.)

I imagine, raising my six sisters and me, even in the era when fathers were much less involved in child rearing than many are today, there must have been days when my dad believed the Catholic church had it right requiring celibacy for it priests. One of those occasions probably followed the story my youngest sister, Susan, told at my father's funeral.

Here are her words. *"My dad was the father of seven daughters. Need I say more? Combining the roles of pastor and father of teenage girls must have been challenging, and we didn't exactly make it easy on him, but he managed to do it with aplomb. One Saturday evening one of his daughters returned home late to find the front door locked. Her date graciously agreed to shimmy up a porch pillar and wake up one of my other sisters to come down and let her in. My father heard knocking and came to investigate. The sister who had been awoken from a sound sleep was not wearing very much. The poor boy scrambled down from the roof, ran to his car, and peeled out of the driveway. The next day, that hapless young man was scheduled to be baptized by immersion, by my father. It is a testament to my dad that he only held that boy under water for a moment longer than necessary."*

This was one of the many dicey occasions that without fanfare Dad coped, unpretentiously meriting his nickname, *"Father Flynn of Girls Town."*

Parents of the 50's and 60's had not lived through the human potential era so they were not as likely to discuss their feelings or encourage their family members to do so either. Parental guidance was based on example and focused more on standards than feelings. Accordingly, my dad, as other well-meaning parents of his time, filled the fatherly role of working hard and providing for his family, as best he could.

To his credit, I have yet to meet many people who had more self-discipline, a better sense of humor, greater humility, or the ability to lead a flock of parishioners and children more gently than he did. I can truthfully say I never heard him raise his voice and towing the line in our household was a way to avoid causing him pain, as opposed to being fearful of repercussions from disobeying him.

When we used to leave the house for an activity or date Dad's typical farewell was: *"Remember whose daughter you are."* To this day, I'm uncertain as to whether he meant that we were to keep in mind that we were the daughters of a minister or to remember we were children of God.

Additionally, he had a great sense of humor; which on more than one occasion was a lifesaver. An interchange I'll never forget occurred when one of my sisters was purchasing a two-piece bathing suit, not, in that era, common attire for a Baptist preacher's daughter. My mother, uncharacteristically abdicating the decision-maker role, informed my sister she had to model the suit for her father before she could wear it out of the house. When my sister came down the stairs clad in her new bathing attire, my father's comment was, *"Well, it's better than nothing."*

Thus, hearing that my father had been admitted to the hospital was shattering news. Because my mom, otherwise self-sufficient, was wheelchair bound, (due to balance issues and severe osteoporosis) it was necessary for one of the seven daughters to promptly return to the parsonage where we were raised, and where my parents resided for the last fifty-six years.

* * *

At that time we, the "seven sandwich-generation daughters," were ages forty-four to fifty-eight and were tied up with our own families and career responsibilities. I was the sole chaplain at a Continuing Care Retirement Community as well as the spiritual coordinator of the Hospice House in Williamsburg, Virginia. My husband was Director of Academic Computing at The College of William and Mary. We were empty nesters and our son was working and living in Las Vegas, Nevada.

Only one of my sisters, Donna, lived in the same state as my parents and she resided two hours away. The rest were unavailable. Linnea was in Hawaii, Susan was vacationing in Florida, Marilee was tied up with family concerns in Florida, Carol, from South Dakota, had been home earlier in the month. Fortunately, Donna was able to immediately come to my parents' aid. However, her window of availability was limited. I had a few more days of vacation before I had to return to work, so my husband

and I decided we'd relieve her by driving to New York the next day.

We arrived at the community hospital to find my dad relatively comfortable enjoying football playoffs with his roommate. He informed my husband and me he was undergoing tests to determine why he was jaundiced, had no appetite, and was losing weight. His spirits were high, he was not in any pain, and he seemed more curious than anxious about being hospitalized.

My mother, who was very outgoing, was conversing with the wife of my dad's roommate. My initial impression was it seemed more like we had walked into a social gathering than a room for sick people.

My second day there my mother and I met with the surgeon who described two non-invasive procedures that had been attempted to diagnose the problem. Unfortunately the first one was unsuccessful because of a blockage. The second one, inserting a tube to drain bile from the liver, was effective for retrieving a sample. Bluntly, the surgeon informed us that there was a 99% chance that my father had pancreatic cancer because they detected a 2-3 centimeter mass at the end of his pancreas blocking his bile duct.

My mother and I were stunned by the news. When our eyes met, I sensed her feelings of disbelief and raw fear. She, who seldom was at a loss for words, seemed incapable of speaking and stared at the doctor.

The surgeon, who was a long-time friend and former parishioner of my dad's, informed Mom and me that the only option available to my father was surgery. He said if surgery were not performed, my dad would die in excruciating pain. He'd been looking at my mother when he issued this curt declaration.

Feeling somewhat railroaded by the limited choices offered - massive surgery or dying in excruciating pain - I responded, *"You are going to do a Whipple on an 87 year old man?"*

The surgeon whipped around to face me, surprised that I knew what surgery he was intending. He then stated, *"Your father's heart and lungs are in good shape, so why wouldn't I perform surgery?"*

I responded, *"After fifteen years working with Hospice and in nursing facilities with the elderly, my experience is that such invasive surgery often causes undue suffering and ends up sacrificing life quality."*

My mid-life career was health-care chaplaincy. By observing situations with individuals in their eighties and older, I realized they typically were balancing chronic and normal aging challenges. Measured and reflective treatment, as opposed to quick intervention, often proved to be most judicious. In other words, for elderly patients, factors other than just tackling the most pressing ailment, no matter how serious, require weighty consideration.

Another course of action for people with serious and chronic illness is palliative care. Palliative care, a relatively recent innovation, focuses on providing relief from the symptoms and stress of chronic illness. Its goal is to provide as much comfort as possible along with maintaining the quality of life. Often that translates to less aggressive treatment and the goal is quality living as opposed to longevity. Palliative care is provided by a team of experts that address not only physical issues but also spiritual and quality of life concerns both for the patient and the caregivers.

I was blindsided by my dad's diagnosis of pancreatic cancer, but in addition to the shock I was feeling, I was troubled by the inevitableness of what seemed like a journey of prescribed anguish. Shouldn't we get a second opinion? Why weren't we being offered the options of other surgeons and venues more sophisticated than this community hospital? It all made me feel as if we were receiving a hurriedly issued ultimatum.

In fifteen years as a Hospice Chaplain, I had seen a number of patients with pancreatic cancer die peacefully, often after a few months of quality living. But, the surgeon's decisive stance coupled with the trusted relationship he had with my parents deterred them from considering alternatives. Though I believed there were choices other than surgery that should have been spelled out for my father, apparently this physician did not. In the circumstances, I felt powerless.

* * *

The totally unexpected diagnosis, pancreatic cancer, sent a shockwave through our family members and friends. Cancer was not a disease that our family had much experience facing. Of the few relatives who'd had it, none of them had cancer of the pancreas. However, I was well aware it carried a very poor prognosis.

Pancreatic cancer was considered terminal, and the surgical treatment for it to prolong the patient's life was the Whipple procedure (a pancreaticoduodenectomy.) During this procedure, surgeons remove the head of the pancreas, a part of the small intestine, a portion of the bile duct, the gallbladder and associated lymph nodes. It is an extremely invasive and complicated procedure and typically only offered in hospitals where specifically trained surgeons and medical personnel are available. It also is often not recommended for elderly patients.

Coincidentally - just after Dad's diagnosis - my sister, Donna, was scheduled to meet with a highly respected gastroenterologist, an appointment she had waited months to get. She had experienced sudden weight loss, and had digestive issues (possibly related to a visit to Mexico), but preliminary tests revealed nothing helpful. At the appointment, she had an interchange with the physician about Dad's issue and the gastroenterologist was surprised a surgeon would consider doing a Whipple on someone Dad's age. The gastroenterologist informed Donna the operation was huge and considered difficult surgery for a 50 year old.

As it turned out the gastroenterologist determined Donna's problem was thyroid related and referred her to an endocrinologist. Donna's treatment protocol prohibited her from being with my parents for the remainder of my Dad's hospital stay, making her grateful that she'd had a chance to be with him when he was initially hospitalized.

After Donna reported what the gastroenterologist said, Linnea, the sister with the most medical expertise, called my father's surgeon. He gave her a detailed explanation of all that had been done thus far regarding my father's treatment, and then explained that the tumor was blocking two important ducts; therefore surgery was the only option. The kind of surgery that would be done, he explained, depended on what he found when he went in. Linnea's reaction to this interchange was: *"I came away from the talk believing that Dad is very fortunate to have Dr. C as his surgeon and friend."*

Linnea's endorsement reinforced my mom's faith that she and my father were making the right decision. So the surgery was scheduled in the local community hospital for the upcoming Monday morning. And while preparations were being made for dad in the hospital, my sisters and I were gearing up to support my mom.

Recognizing the criticalness of this surgery, four of my sisters arranged to come home and be present to my parents and each other. My husband and I, however, could not remain there for the surgery; we had to return to our work in Virginia.

While the surgery preparations were being finalized, Dad was undergoing testing. There were some professionals at the hospital intimating that the resources of this community hospital might not be the best match for such comprehensive surgery, but my parents trust in and longtime friendship with the surgeon trumped the request for a second opinion or advocating for a hospital transfer.

Less than twelve hours before his surgery was scheduled to begin, while my father was visiting with two of my sisters, the attending anesthesiologist paid Dad a visit. He stated he had concerns about Dad's fitness for serious surgery. He questioned my father about his ability to climb stairs and asked if there was someone to vouch for the health of his heart. Though this interaction was profoundly disconcerting to my sisters who were present, my father apparently somewhat nonchalantly responded to his concerns in a manner that satisfied the doctor, and he remained part of the surgery team.

In predicaments such as this, one of the greatest challenges is confronting the uncertainties. There is no way of knowing how my dad would fare, the long-term ramifications, or the latitude of time involved in his requiring care. The surgeon had informed my father that following the operation, my father should expect to spend a few days in the Intensive Care Unit, and a couple of weeks recuperating in the hospital before his return home.

Often individuals facing critical surgery focus on the most immediate concern, living through the surgery. Other ramifications such as the significant loss in strength and mobility, from being bed-bound for a lengthy period, and the work and time involved in getting back to an acceptable level of independence aren't considered. Our family realized that even if recovery occurred as the surgeon predicted, with my mother wheelchair bound, help would be needed on the home front for an extended period of time.

Fortunately for my parents and the remaining six sisters, Carol, my South Dakota sister, volunteered, after hearing the prognosis, to take a family leave and move in with my parents for at least a month. Thankfully, and with no cajoling, one immediate stressor had been overcome. Now my mother, who competently oversaw the household, would not have to worry about someone transporting her, (and her wheelchair,) to visit my dad. This was a major relief to her at a very stressful time.

* * *

Because I had pressing obligations at work and no one to cover for me, I had to sit out the surgery in Virginia. My feelings about not sharing the vigil with the family members who were able to be present were mixed. I sensed this operation was not going to be as straightforward as our family had been led to believe. And no matter how successful the operation was, I, having visited fragile, elderly patients in early recovery from acute surgery, felt somewhat relieved to not bear witness to my father enduring a level of suffering that would be heartbreaking.

Did I feel guilt? Yes. But watching helplessness, a body hooked up to every manner of tube, and mental confusion all are painful to observe, and more so with someone you love. I also was aware that this was just the beginning of, at best, an extended recuperation or, at worst, a long drawn-out time of dying.

Despite sharing the burden of parental support with six sisters, which seems more than adequate, I recognized our caregiving resources would have to be rationed, and undoubtedly my turn to be present would be of greater value down the road. But despite these pressures, it was tough not being able to share that critical time with my family. The morning of the surgery, I made the following journal entry:

Today's the day, as Donna elucidated, that Daddy gets gutted. How can I get over my feeling that because of the availability of a surgeon, Mommy and Daddy are so fond of and who they trust unreservedly, not all options, i.e. comfort care, were explored?

It's been mind-boggling to me how paralyzing this situation is to my ability to go about my daily routine. My concentration seems to have left or be leaving me half the time. And worst of all the train is just leaving the station.

That evening I received word that the surgical procedure had taken six and a half hours and the surgeon believed he was successful in removing the entire tumor. After a time in the recovery room, Dad was transported to the Intensive Care Unit. After briefly seeing him in Intensive Care, Mom, who was utterly spent, went home to bed.

I breathed a sigh of relief when I got the good news that the surgery had gone well. But, as reports from my sisters were delivered, I experienced a gamut of emotions: guilt for not being present, anguish imagining what this was like for my dad and my mother, and fear of what the future would bring.

A practice I had begun over two decades earlier to cope with life's pressure was jogging. Part of my early morning ritual on weekdays was running 3-5 miles. When my son was young, he validated its effectiveness in my life because occasionally when I was apparently less than calm, he'd ask, *"Do you think you need to go for a run?"*

Thankfully during this time of stress I had my outlet of running to help me cope. And though I wasn't on site with the drama, my sisters who were, kept the rest of us informed; as you'll see from Susan's description during the day that followed the surgery.

Daddy seemed to know someone was there when we visited him in the ICU but he is really not noticeably aware. The nurses say he is still in critical condition but stable....He remains in the limbo state. He is a bit swollen, especially in hands and neck areas. (He looks like the cousin to the incredible hulk.) He is on a respirator and will continue to be as it has something to do with the pain medication and how it is being administered. They say he needs to remain on the respirator and in this state to heal. (He has every conceivable tube connected to him.)

My sisters, even those who had returned home, were all "bone" tired from their ordeal. Susan's email after getting home directed at Carol, the caregiver, was:

Several people told me today that I "looked like crap." (Perhaps it was the haircut you gave me, Carol??) My boss said I looked very tired, and then he said it was a good thing I came back to work so I could rest! I think of you all often."

Though my father's illness dominated our attention, routine life wasn't on hold for any of us. All of us were working and the five younger sisters all had parenting responsibilities, with children still at home. Donna was coping with her own medical issues and Marilee, not only singly parenting her six children, was also sole proprietor of a frame shop.

It wasn't until a week after the surgery that there was any encouraging news; finally Dad's respirator was removed. The nurse present for the procedure, when the tube was removed, reported that for a few moments Dad was very alert and his first words were, *"Am I free to go now?"* Sadly, no one knows if this was his famous sense of humor kicking in or if he was, at some level, sensing deliverance. Later that day, after dauntlessly navigating stormy winter weather, my mother and Carol arrived at the hospital and found him sleeping fitfully. But, as he drifted in and out of consciousness, he was asking questions, such as, *"What happened? Why am I here? Have I been hijacked?"*

At the time of my dad's illness my mother was in her early eighties. Though physically frail, she did not lack skills in maintaining a household, decision-making, and getting her needs met. She'd always demonstrated strength in facing life's challenges, and she faced my dad's illness with a practical stoicness. However, seeing her helpmate of sixty years confused and critically ill, and living with the uncertainty of how this would be resolved, took its toll on her.

In addition to all she was doing, Carol faithfully wrote daily email bulletins. Often these reports were disheartening but they were sustenance to my soul. I discovered being informed of the realities of Dad's day-to-day life, no matter how depressing, was less wearing than groundless speculation. Concentrating on my own responsibilities was challenging enough without unsubstantiated thoughts of my dad's condition in the Intensive Care Unit creeping into my imagination. Because I couldn't be present, I was unspeakably grateful for Carol's sacrifice and presence.

* * *

Looming on the horizon was the knowledge that once Dad was transferred to a regular hospital bed from the ICU unit, not only would he be more aware, but also his needs would not be met as attentively. So, we began making plans to have another one of us staffing the home-front along with Carol so one person would be present with Dad at the hospital as much as possible, and the other sister could be available to chauffeur mom and run errands.

In this day and age hospitalizations involve numerous procedures, many of which are intricate and complicated by varying medical professionals working different shifts, so there's a lot to keep straight. Most physicians will counsel family members about hospital patients, particularly those who cannot speak for themselves, to try and have someone available by the bedside as much as possible. Nursing staff workloads are heavy, precluding time to attend to non-medical concerns that can play a significant role in comfort and recovery.

I hated the thought of my dad being alone in the hospital, needing help and having no one present to attend to his needs. I also thought about the loneliness and despair hospital patients often experienced, wondering if anyone cared and suffering anxious thoughts regarding the uncertainty of the future. Added to this was the guilt I felt attending to my patients in Williamsburg when I couldn't be available to my own father and family.

Arranging coverage and having enough days in a row without obligations to make a trip to New York was difficult for me because not only was I the sole chaplain in a 380 person retirement community, but I also served ten hours a week as chaplain at our local Hospice House. It was an ongoing challenge to balance my obligations to my "parishioner" patients and residents, with my particular commitment to my own family. It was hard to process the feelings associated with tending to the sick of my ministry arena while my father was seriously ill elsewhere. The tension between work and family is universal, but my work embodied my father's suffering, so I felt everyone's pain twofold.

Originally, the surgeon said that my father would probably be in the hospital for two weeks post surgery, but after his first week recovering in ICU, it was inconceivable that a discharge could happen anytime soon.

"Uncharted territory," became the expression we used for the medical course we all had embarked on with our father. In uncharted territory, he vacillated in and out of consciousness and sense-making, One nurse explained to my sister that it often takes awhile for anesthesia to wear off after surgery. I remembered several years earlier, after my father underwent outpatient hernia surgery, that he reported it was six months before he felt like himself. So this time, when he was more debilitated going in and having a more prolonged surgery, one could only imagine how long recovery might take.

In several emails Carol reported that Daddy, *"is not the man I remember but there are definite signs of his old self breaking through."* She also remembered a lesson we all need to take to heart: In such situations often one's worst personality traits are magnified and one's true character shows through. Though my father had little tolerance for discomfort and did not always show enthusiasm for what he was asked to do, like breathing treatments, he was never anything but polite, grace-filled and grateful in his interactions with his caregivers.

* * *

While my father's hospital existence went on, life continued for me. Being hundreds of miles away from this anguishing drama was difficult, although being present, I imagined, was probably equally insufferable. Each day I keenly anticipated news of the latest development that often made me both laugh and cry. One day Carol reported:

Daddy was sleeping when I arrived so I sat in a chair and read for while. Every time he wakes up he looks intently at you, and when he recognizes you, he smiles a big smile and says 'Oh hi' or something nice. It makes you feel like a million bucks just for being there.

Because we knew those "feeling like a million bucks" experiences were few and far between and because we were in awe of Carol's stamina and endurance when coping with our parents, we consistently stated our gratefulness.

Thanks, wrote Susan to Carol, *so much for being there at this most stressful and difficult time. It won't last forever and someday you will be able to look back at it as a memory. Keep chanting that to yourself to help you get through, you saint.*

Eventually in the next post surgery days, Dad's nasogastric tube, (the tube that goes from the stomach out through the nose) was removed and he had his first sip of water; the restraints (a circumstance I cannot tolerate thinking about for anyone) were removed and Dad recognized Mom, Carol, the surgeon and the nurses. All seemed pleased with these indicators of progress and Daddy began sporadically exhibiting interest in his visitors, the news and other television shows.

Negotiating medical territory is like riding a roller coaster. One day the report was that Dad was being denied water both because he could not keep it down and there were no indications of bowel sounds. Another day, he slept almost the entire day and was not able to identify his visitors. One of my sisters responded to that report with the following:

Hang in there, Carol. It has to be so bizarre to see Daddy missing the one thing we could always count on him to have—his rock-solid and dazzlingly brilliant marbles. It's only temporary. It's only temporary. ....

Another day when Dad was more lucid and my mom and sister were present the surgeon visited and informed Daddy that he'd undergone a huge operation and he was a hero. *"No one,"* the surgeon commented, *"had ever had that big of an operation in this hospital."* My humble, respectful father responded that congratulations were due to him, the surgeon, not the patient.

My reaction to hearing this was twofold. It reinforced the pride I had in my father's character. He never took undue credit and he was always quick to commend others. My other reaction confirmed my suspicion that this surgery was not one routinely (or ever) performed in this hospital.

Faced with imminent surgery, particularly when the need for it arises out of the blue, patients often focus on actually having it performed, rather than the expertise of the surgeon or the level of capability of the medical facility to handle the specific operation. The convenience of already being a patient in the facility where a surgeon is offering his or her services, almost always trumps getting a second opinion or searching for an environment where the staff is specifically trained to care for, in this case, post-Whipple patients.

* * *

After spending two weeks in the Intensive Care Unit Dad was transferred to a step-down room, which signaled the call for the sister rotation machine to send in reinforcements. I was amazed and relieved by how well Carol was holding out but I recognized she was in need of a break when she mentioned in an email that it was good Linnea was arriving because, *"a person can take just so much!"*

The report, after the move to the step-down unit, was that Dad was profoundly weak, his albumin level was life-threatening (because of severe malnutrition) and he was retaining fluid. In spite of his conditions, he was being urged to sit up, something he had not done since his surgery. And sitting upright was just one of a continuing sequence of activities that he was being pushed to do. Eating and drinking were insufferable for him, breathing treatments were difficult, and he was so weak any movement required excruciating effort.

Linnea, taking the first turn of sister reinforcements was with him the day he stated, *"I can't go on like this."* Fortunately being a professor of psychiatric nursing she had the wherewithal to respond, *"No, you can't, but you won't have to because things won't stay like this."*

Being in such intensely intimate and painful places with one's parents is not a situation any of us had previously experienced; nor is it something many are prepared to encounter. It's akin to finding yourself in a foreign land where much of what you know and believe, is turned on its head, and you are unfamiliar with the language to even communicate, but you have no choice but to soldier on as best you can.

My dad was not regaining his strength because he either could not take in adequate nutrition, or it was not being absorbed into his system. Eating was an effort and his ability to tolerate food waned. The surgeon strongly and consistently reiterated to him that he had to eat, that food was medicine. On more than one occasion the surgeon himself actually spoon-fed his hero patient.

After another episode, when the surgeon insisted he eat, my sister Linnea initiated a serious discussion with Dad letting him know that it was his choice to eat and exert himself or not. If eating and exertion were so agonizing that the effort to do so destroyed his quality of life, it was his right to stop doing them.

Apparently at least at some level he wasn't ready to stop, because in the next few days Dad exerted himself more, exercising his feet, sitting up, tolerating the breathing exercises better, etc. The eating continued to be terribly challenging and discomforting and the pureed food or *"moosh"* as Carol designated it certainly did not help. Even with not doing much physically, the majority of his days were spent sleeping.

Much to the collective relief of my mother and sisters, Carol, without any persuading on anyone's part, decided that she would extend her leave of absence from her teaching job in South Dakota and continue with her caregiving role at the parsonage in New York. But before she could do so, she needed a weeklong break to return home to see her family and attend to business.

Before I had time to think about whether or not I could arrange time off from work to cover her break, Annilee and Susan agreed to return. Because by now, four weeks after major surgery, Dad was no longer in upgraded care it was important to have a family member with him as much as possible.

* * *

During their visit, Annilee and Susan became acquainted with the daily onslaught of interruptions by the staff that provided medical care, meals, and routine tests ordered by the physician. Thus, when a worker came in and informed them they were taking Dad for a procedure, they were surprised and asked Dad if he knew what this was about. He responded that the surgeon had mentioned he was going to do some procedure but my father wasn't worried about *IT* because he stated, *"IT doesn't involve cutting."*

Before they wheeled him to his destination, my father was informed that they needed his consent because the procedure might involve "re-routing of some tubes." Because of everyone's trust and faith in the surgeon, my Ivy League educated sisters--one of whom is an attorney, and the other who was high school valedictorian--had no reason to question what was going on, even though at this point it was questionable if my father would have been deemed capable of making any medical decisions.

Fifteen years previously, in 1991, the *Patient Self-Determination Act,* passed by the federal government, went into effect, which states that *everyone has the right to refuse or accept care, and all patients over 18 must be given information they need to, make an "informed decision."* Basically as a result of this act surgeons and physicians are required to carefully explain the procedures they are proposing for patients before they actually do them. Once the patient is given the explanation, signing the form is an indication not only that the patient is giving permission for the procedure, but also that he/she understands what exactly the procedure entails. In cases either where the patient is unable to make the decision, or incapable of comprehending the information, the signature of the health care power of attorney is required.

An hour and ten minutes *after* the procedure began the surgeon gave my sisters the explanation for the surgery. He said that he had replaced the tube that was acting as Dad's bile duct, bringing the bile from the liver to the intestine, and he had rerouted another tube that had been on his right side so he could be fed through it. (Though disguised by the surgeon's explanation, the reality was my father now had a permanent feeding tube, a medical state of affairs expressly prohibited in his living will.)

My sisters, focusing on my father's immediate comfort after this procedure, and believing the surgeon was just doing what he had to do in the circumstances, did not really take in all the ramifications of this development. A feeding tube! However, when I heard about the presence of a permanent feeding tube and the cavalier manner in which it was done, along with not involving the family or offering a choice, I was stunned. Inserting a feeding tube is a huge undertaking, not something a medical professional should decide to have inserted without full disclosure to family and consent from a capable patient or advocate.

Many states now have advance directives available primarily for fragile elderly patients that not only specify a person's wishes regarding resuscitation but also intubation, feeding tubes and even antibiotics. Feeding tubes are considered to be extraordinary measures. People should be offered the opportunity not only to consent to their insertion but also to how long they want them operative.

Feeling totally powerless, four hundred miles away, and aware the deed had been done, I held my counsel. Everyone else, with the exception of one sister who conversed with me about this, seemed to take this development in stride as just one more essential development in this nightmarish journey.

* * *

A reason the insertion of a feeding tube is a big deal is it triggers a course of action that often puts patients on a slippery slope where more and more life-sustaining treatment becomes difficult to avoid. It also can cause increased suffering. That is what occurred in my father's case. Yes, he would continue to exist, but his life would involve ongoing challenges including inability to enjoy eating, incontinence, and nausea. That day, however, no one thought about the big picture because there were immediate concerns.

My sisters reported: *We asked the surgeon if we could give Dad water, as his throat is very dry. He said yes as long as he was sitting up and alert. They are fearful that if his swallowing mechanism is not working correctly that he will get fluid in his lungs.*

The first thing Dad asked for after the procedure was water. Susan promised to give him some. When we got upstairs the nurse said we could do it only if the written orders said we could do it. We did it anyway, as we had promised him, and the surgeon said we could. Dad took some in, but also spit up a lot of green solid gunk, that looked like half chewed broccoli, right into Susan's hand! It was a little scary to see him cough like that. But after that little bit of water, his voice sounded great! Just like his old self. His throat has been so parched.

Dad seemed quite alert. When we told him his voice sounded great, he said he had to speak in an hour in Nyack. We thought he was making a joke, but then he said other stuff that made us think he was NOT joking. At one point, he asked when he was going to be taken to his bed. We said that he was in bed. Later I asked the nurse if the sedatives he was given for the procedure could have caused his confusion and she said, "Yes."

He did know Susan and me and said to a nurse that he had wonderful daughters. He most certainly was NOT confused about that!

The nurse said that feeding him directly into the intestines often perks patients up after a day or two, so let us hope that is the case. My impressions of dad's condition kept changing. I went from thinking that he was very weak to seeing him quite alert and engaged, to seeing him confused and disoriented. It is very hard to know what course this will take at this point.

Despite the feeding tube Dad did not gain strength and continued to want to sleep almost continuously. In his waking times, which were few and far between, he was relatively aware of what was transpiring but the persistent reports were of him being worn-out.

* * *

An excerpt from a few days later.

The perkiest that I (Susan) saw Dad all day happened when Carol walked in around 5:00. She had come to pick up Annilee and Mommy, and when she said hello to him, his face really brightened up and he spoke more than I had seen him speak all day. He seems to regard Carol as the person he should report to—as someone who is really interested in him and his progress, and perhaps to whom he feels accountable (imagine that!). Right away he told her that he had sat up for over an hour that morning, and then he told her about the procedure that he had had the day before and how awful it was. But he also said that they had apparently gotten something good done during it, so he felt that at least that was good. (Obviously either he had not been educated or he was incapable of remembering it involved a feeding tube.)

Unfortunately the food he was getting in his tube was giving him diarrhea so they tried diluting the contents with water. Getting diarrhea is really problematic because he is still too weak to use a bedpan, but sadly he seems oblivious to the mess he is making.

Part of the roller coaster was Dad stating he was losing a sense of time. For a man who took his watch to the repair shop if it was off a minute a day, who knew to the minute how much time it took to go anywhere, whose life was dictated by a clock, this was big and terribly frustrating. During this time he often forgot who visited him, and sometimes did not recognize his visitors.

In the next day or so he was moved to a private room because it was determined he had an infection. Then on the heels of that, word was out that his discharge was imminent – which sent mom into a tailspin.

After talking with the surgeon it was learned a discharge is imminent but they definitely will keep Daddy hospitalized over the weekend. Apparently the surgeon remarked that since Dad had been a patient since Christmas week, over a month, the pressure was on to discharge.

We appreciate this time with Daddy and can see that he really is doing what he can. It is just that it is uncharted territory and no one knows what he can and cannot actually do. When we asked him if he were bored he said not really, just very very tired and that is obvious. But...his old self is peeking through!

In our current medical environment, physicians are held hostage by insurance guidelines in determining the lengths of hospitalizations for various illnesses. With the excessive cost of hospital care, patients are at the mercy of their funding source and often forced out of the hospital when they are extremely vulnerable. We were fearful that would happen to Dad.

* * *

A month had past since Dad's surgery and my sisters and I discussed how we felt - like we were flying by the seat of our pants. Our feelings vacillated between uncertainty, fear and small measures of hope. Not that there's much choice to do otherwise, but we were doing our best to take things as they came because no one knew what would come next.

For me being miles from the actual daily events was frustrating but with only a limited number of days available I could be away from my job, and knowing my sisters were covering, I felt it best to save the vacation time I did have and use it to be with him when he was no longer hospitalized.

Fortunately, though her communications were disturbing to me, my sister kept me posted by email, which helped bridge, the gap when I could not be present.

Dad's condition is heartbreaking. He is completely helpless. He doesn't even know when he poops and it seems he poops all of the time. Yesterday he thought he smelled some cooking when what he smelled was his poop!

I never know what to expect when I walk in that hospital room. Sometimes he is so terribly weak and out of it and other times he seems almost chipper. It is emotionally exhausting.

Dad's imminent discharge was postponed because the surgeon felt he needed another swallow evaluation, and he wanted to be present for it. Several conversations took place between the surgeon and my mom and the sisters present. The surgeon said Dad has the kind of cancer that can come back. If it does, then radiation and chemotherapy would be treatment options. He also said that chemotherapy is not particularly effective for this kind of cancer so he is not recommending it. He is not bringing this up to Dad at this time but he wanted mom to know this.

This is the first time that the doctor talked in a way that sounded like he was trying to prepare us for his death. It was very emotional.

Of course, when I received this report, it brought a watershed of tears. Though I had companioned others through extended illnesses when it was unclear if the person would live or not, seeing my own father go through it was heartrending. In addition to the pain I was feeling for my dad and mom, I realized I had some questions. We had never formally gotten a report about the cancer itself. Neither, to my knowledge, had an oncologist ever been brought in to consult.

Ironically when many families are going through equivalent nightmares, numerous physicians are involved.

There's the hospitalist, the surgeon, an oncologist, and often other specialists like cardiologists and other physicians involved. As a result the challenge often is getting the various physicians to talk to each other so they can be encouraged to view the patient as a whole human being instead of as a fragmented one; a heart or cancer or kidney patient. In this situation, the surgeon was singularly directing our father's treatment.

Physicians have varying styles in relating to patients and families. One style, that used to be predominate, is authoritarian – these doctors pretty much inform patients as to what they will be doing. Obviously this was the case here, but this was my parents' maiden voyage through the muddle of serious illness, and they did not know that some doctors offer a more collegial style where there is more interaction and family involvement when there are serious decisions to be made. Seemingly, because my parents had such a close relationship with the surgeon and because he was a member of my dad's church, a greater understanding of physician styles would not have changed things. My parents trusted their friend implicitly, and they followed his lead without questioning or considering alternatives, believing it would be rude and offensive to do otherwise.

There are patients and families who prefer the authoritarian approach. A number of years ago I was in the hospital room with a couple that heralded from the Greatest Generation. After graduating from West Point

Military Academy, the husband, who was also the patient, had enjoyed a stellar military career; rising to the level of General.

When their cardiologist walked in the room, the couple invited me to remain and hear the report of results of tests that had been administered. The physician offered the couple several treatment options: handle problem with prescription medication, operate, or wait and see without doing anything. After the cardiologist left the room, General C turned to me and said, *"I want the doctor to tell me what to do; I do not want to tell him what he should do."* Possibly my parents felt the same way.

No one in our family doubted that the surgeon was giving what he believed to be his all to this case. We were affirmed in this conviction because on more than one occasion, hospital personnel commented that my father must be someone special for the surgeon to give him so much attention. His friend, the surgeon, truly had my father's best interests at heart, although I couldn't help wondering how, without having a conversation and actually listening to my father, he could know what my dad wanted in all this. It was obvious, success to the surgeon meant prolonging life at all costs, which trumped considering what his patient considered quality of living.

* * *

For a number of years my dad had been suffering from nausea and dizziness, conditions that seriously impacted his enjoyment of life. Also he had recently been diagnosed with diabetes, probably related to this pancreatic tumor. Though he had significant patience when it came to dealing with individuals religiously, along with other aspects of his profession, he possessed little tolerance for discomfort or the demands of unfamiliar situations. In the circumstances, he either did not want or was unable to manage his diabetes and medication regime and abdicated responsibility to my mother. In the midst of this medical crisis, his challenges with persistent nausea and dizziness were not considered, and though the interventions he received were performed with good intentions, they appeared more reactionary than measured or reflective.

* * *

And so the saga continued. Still hospitalized more than a month after surgery when two sisters arrived for an evening visit, Dad's greeting was, *"This has been hell. I have had a pain in my side. This is hell. Who is running this contest?"*

My sister described her encounter. *The poor man was very frustrated and agitated. Annilee explained that it was 6:30 p.m. and she had left at 3:00 and he didn't have the pain then. This calmed him down. Obviously it was very frustrating for him losing his sense of time.*

She sat and held Dad's hand and talked to him. She sympathized with him and asked if he ever prays. He said that he often feels too weak to pray even though he wants to. She then said that even if he is too weak to pray there are many people praying for him. He then said that sometimes he feels like praying that God will take him home with him. Annilee said that was very understandable and that Mr. Brown, (a close family friend), had felt that way when he was very ill.

Later we talked about how all the sisters had been to see him and how we write emails to each other about him and that we all love him. He said, "I was not a perfect father."

Carol's response, "Well, we were not perfect daughters."

That comment triggered hilarity when I read that email. What an understatement - especially because the daughter who proclaimed it would have won the contest, hands down among all of us, for exemplifying the greatest parental challenges. An example of one of those challenges was at age 17 (fortunately after she completed high school) Carol embarked on a bicycle trip cross-country with two boys and abandoned them to settle in South Dakota, where she eventually got college and masters degrees, married (more than once) and raised six children. Now, ironically, she'd turned into a candidate for canonization.

As often was the case, in addition to the laughter the reports generated, they engendered emotional pain, the pain we all were feeling that Susan's response to Annilee captured well.

Annilee you are amazing. I don't know how you could have a talk like that without totally breaking down but it is wonderful that you could say and do those things with Dad. I am sitting at my desk at work crying just reading your report. Thanks for keeping us so informed. I really appreciate your taking the time to write such good accounts. I know how tired one is after returning home from the hospital at night. It is a real effort of love for you to take the time and energy to write us an email after such difficult days.

Amidst the heart-breaking narratives were also ones that made us laugh, and raised our spirits. Our father chuckled when Carol said she knew someone who called Meals on Wheels, *"Yuk from the Truck."*

On another occasion Dad informed his surgeon that he had a sensation in his stomach that made him feel like he is having a baby. That gave the surgeon pause. He just didn't quite know how to react when his patient chose to describe his symptoms in a manner that was a medical impossibility.

One day my mother coughed and dad joked, *"Do you need a tube down your throat?"* When Carol informed him we referred to him as Jack because he is like a Jack in the box – he has his ups and downs, he *retorted, "Don't you mean 'Jackass'?"*

That was an uncharacteristic remark for our father, the gentleman. Probably the only occasion we'd heard him use the word *ass* previously was when he was reading the Palm Sunday story about Jesus from the King James Version of the Bible.

When his former associate pastor came to visit at the hospital and said a prayer with him, Dad tenderly commented to those in the room, *"Now you can see why I asked Hank to be my associate."* Reading about that interchange put a lump in my throat. It was affirmation the father I loved was still with us.

Reading these daily messages from the sisters stationed on the home front caused various reactions from laughter, to sadness, to hope and often to frustration. I detested the image of my dignified gentlemanly father being subjected to the indecencies of incontinence and confinement to bed when two months earlier he had been writing, cooking, walking and enjoying meals with friends and family.

Often I'd be walking the hallway on the way to make a visit in my retirement community and memories of my father preaching at the pulpit, conducting a wedding ceremony or briskly striding up our street would come to mind. The sorrow I'd feel - recognizing these times would probably be no more - brought tears to my eyes.

My feelings cycled from guilt, for not being there with him, fear for how our family would handle what lay ahead, and hopelessness for his plight. Absorbing myself in my professional responsibilities and being several hundred miles away, distracted me from these emotions much of the time. However, periodically I was blindsided by grief when I visited patients in comparable situations.

* * *

The final days of hospitalization were very tense due in part to the fact that the discharge planners kept announcing and then postponing Dad's discharge. Linnea was coordinating with the staff for a transition to a nursing facility. Dad seemed to take in that he would be leaving the hospital and relocated to a nursing home but it was difficult to tell exactly what this meant to him because his reaction seemed to be resigned apathy.

A condition patients who have been away from their familiar surroundings often suffer is called *transfer trauma*. Transfer trauma is basically the stress a person experiences when moved from a familiar to a strange environment. Elderly and frail individuals are particularly susceptible and the trauma can be exacerbated by visual or hearing impairment and cognitive deficiencies, and more than one move. Effects of the stress hamper recovery and in many cases result in confusion, depression, anxiety, anger, fear and helplessness. At times various behaviors like withdrawal, aggression, crying, and manipulation manifest.

My father certainly appeared to be suffering from the effects of his now six-week institutionalization. He often referred to the hospital as an *"eerie place,"* or in his worst moments, *a prison, a place where they have their tricks right and left.* And he mentioned that the crew was inefficient.

One day when my mother was trying to comfort him with scripture, she quoted, *"Delight thyself in the Lord and he will give thee the desires of thine heart,"* Dad said that that verse seemed hard to believe at this time.

Despite that, Dad was making minimal progress physically. His strength increased negligibly, he passed his swallow evaluation and actually took two steps with the physical therapist. Though extremely taxing physically, doing so gave him hope that he might be capable of walking again.

Living in a Nursing Facility

When we received the definitive date that Dad would be discharged I arranged a trip home. The discharge plan was for my father to be transferred to a local nursing facility for rehabilitation. There are specific Medicare guidelines specifying who is eligible for rehab services and the length of time Medicare subsidizes it. The goal is for the patient to eventually return to the level of independence they were at, prior to their hospitalization.

Since my profession involved working in a retirement community that had a convalescent and rehab center, I was well aware of the unfortunate realities involved in everyday life in a nursing home setting, along with the challenges of transitioning to live in a total care facility. I anticipated this would be a trying time for my parents; and my caring husband, (who when he married me had no idea he would be married to a minister, but without whose support, I could not imagine being one), offered to accompany me. However, realizing this was not a convenient time for him to be away from work, and aware he wasn't really needed, we decided I would travel alone.

I left my home in Williamsburg at 4:00 a.m. on my dad's discharge day, and arrived - somewhat shell shocked from the grueling drive - at his hospital room six hours later. Annilee was there with my father, and a nurse was scurrying around preparing him for his wheelchair ambulance ride to the nursing facility. Though he had a wide smile and gave me a hearty welcome, it was obvious he had lost a lot of weight in the six weeks since I'd seen him. He asked me about my trip and my husband and thanked me for coming. It was my first experience actually seeing my father so helpless and frail, and though I had anticipated it, the reality was shocking and painful. I watched while two people transferred him to the wheelchair.

My father's transport, a bumpy and uncomfortable ambulance ride, went without incident. Fortuitously, at the nursing facility he was assigned to one of the few single rooms, probably due to his having a feeding tube and related toileting issues. Despite having privacy, the environment was anything but uplifting. It was very much a traditional nursing home with a long hall strewn with wheelchair bound residents, many of them making moaning sounds; the epitome of a place you hope you never have to send a loved one.

Our father was not one to directly express his feelings so his way to convey his relief, at finally leaving the hospital after almost seven weeks, and to bolster our spirits, was to crack some jokes which gave us hope that his old self was returning. One was regarding his food intake. Even with his feeding tube, he was encouraged to eat orally both for pleasure (how can pureed foods be pleasurable?) and to ensure his swallowing got stronger. He had finally begun feeding himself and Carol, who was keeping him company while he ate, said, *"I love the way that food is going down."* He responded, *"Then stick around and you will see it come up."*

I had brought several eight by ten framed pictures of our family to display in Dad's room, one of them a recent picture of his seven daughters. Not only are personal items comforting to the resident during their stay, but also they serve as conversational prompts for staff and visitors. My father loved telling people he had seven daughters, was known as "Father Flynn of Girls' Town", and that he appreciated the male box outside his home. But no amount of humor was sufficient to invalidate the pain that admission to a nursing facility was causing all of us. My mom's sadness was evident and Dad appeared despondent.

Something I had learned as a chaplain was there are times when rather than trying to raise someone's spirits, particularly someone who has justification for feeling low, it is more beneficial to encourage them to rant out all the frustrations and pains inherent in their experience. It is like accompanying someone while they are climbing down into a pit. In most cases, they will in essence reach bottom, and once their pain has been spoken and heard, without prompting, they will lead you up, maybe only a step or two, from the bottom of the pit, by naming a silver lining in their situation.

On this occasion, it might have been therapeutic to have said to my father, *"Being in a nursing facility is the pits. It's nothing like being home, is it?"* He might then have felt free to express his negative feelings.

However, with individuals such as my father who seldom expressed personal feelings, especially if they were negative, this technique might not be effective. I do wish that I had offered him the invitation but at the time it was easier to protect my mother and sister, from the pain of him describing his misery.

I did hope he would find the support in that facility, as he needed to become stronger and return to some measure of independence. His major accomplishment in the hospital was gaining the strength to sit up for more than an hour so I wondered how, in his fragile and weakened state, he'd handle the required physical therapy, which would be much more demanding. His garb in the hospital had been degrading opened back hospital gowns and possibly graduating to house coats and sweat pants would raise his spirits.

The underlying issue was food absorption. Even with the feeding tube he was not getting the nourishment he needed. My sister Susan's comment to this was that it occurred to her that our family's traditional pre-meal prayer, that had come to sound perfunctory, (*Please bless this food to our bodies*) had never been so meaningful.

After only the first two days, Dad told me he was reluctant to push his call button because he never likes to ask for things for himself. He mentioned that he didn't want to be a bother but also the response time is so slow, it seems futile. I encouraged him to use the bell, that's why they supplied him with it, though it must be frustrating to not know if anyone will even respond. At least he had a phone so he could make calls and our family members could call him when we couldn't be there.

Because Dad was more aware he also was more miserable lying in bed. He stated to my mother that he was feeling like a prisoner. Then he asked a question, which was heart wrenching, "*Did Mr. M stop eating because he just couldn't take it anymore?*" My mother replied, "*Yes. But you are not at that point yet.*"

Though I chose not to speak my thoughts aloud, I would have liked to ask my mother how she was able to know what point my dad was at? Maybe he was trying to tell us he just couldn't or didn't want to take what was happening anymore. He certainly was acknowledging his misery and in retrospect I wish I'd found a way to pursue those feelings rather than being complicit in shutting them down.

It hurts to be in the presence of someone who is acknowledging their anguish, but granting that person the opportunity and a safe place to verbalize what they are feeling is a great gift. What often complicates our ability to receive their feelings, is that doing so intensifies our own level of pain. Understandably, in this case, the thought of my father intentionally not eating was more than my mother could endure.

Since my dad had only been in this rehab environment for two days we hoped that when the therapy actually started it would help him sleep well at night; the time he seemed most vulnerable to loneliness. So far, at the facility, his appetite remained poor and he ate just a few spoonfuls at each meal, possibly because he was afraid either of choking or regurgitating. The whole situation was miserable.

My third day in New York I awoke to eight inches of snow. This was very disappointing because instead of visiting my dad, I spent the morning shoveling the driveway. I also chose to heed the warning of the police to refrain from driving unless it was an emergency situation. I felt particularly sorry for my dad because it was Sunday, and often in medical facilities weekends seem more drawn out because so little is going on.

My sister, who was housebound with me, called and asked Dad if he watched the preacher Joel Osteen on TV, a program he had previously watched religiously, and he said, *"I am not ready for his optimistic outlook right now."* We felt so sad for him but were grateful he admitted to a small extent how he felt. He stated that the aids were very long in coming in to clean him up but knew they probably were short staffed because of the storm. Then he added facetiously, *"Their lateness will be rewarded with a big smell."*

I was appalled by the deterioration in my father's quality of life, from dignified independent living to bed-bound requiring total care and now existing in a rehabilitation center where he struggled with continence issues. For me one of the most difficult aspects of working in a retirement community is witnessing the decline of vibrant, independent residents as they cope with physical and mental challenges of aging. But seeing these changes happen quickly in someone you love is even more devastating.

Before my visit to New York ended, and because no one at the facility had broached the topic, I decided to talk with my father about a, *"Do Not Resuscitate Order."* New York State law dictated that unless he and a physician had signed a form saying he did not want to be resuscitated, if he stopped breathing, or his heart stopped beating, a medical professional would initiate cardiopulmonary resuscitation (CPR). I felt it was important to find out if that was his wish, particularly because of the statements he'd been making about how he wasn't sure he could go on this way.

I chose a time for the conversation when no other family members were around. Though my mother agreed this conversation needed to take place, she did not want to be present. I'd had similar discussions with many individuals in a professional capacity, but it felt uncomfortable raising this issue with my own father. Though both of us were aware of the seriousness of the interchange, and that it was occurring at a time when his health was precarious, my father did not hesitate to sign officially that should his heart stop beating and he stop breathing, that he not be resuscitated. Rather matter of factly, without comment, he completed the form. My reaction was I had one less item to be anxious about because now my dad's wishes in this regard were known and they could be honored. Also I was relieved by his choice because I knew that statistically, very few frail elderly individuals who were resuscitated were able afterwards to return to independent living.

* * *

A typical day in the rehabilitation facility seemed to be one without much happening, but was actually packed with constant little intrusions – swallow therapy, cleanups, physical and occupational therapy and social visits. Still extremely weak, Dad's body was not absorbing the nutrition it needed so his physical therapy sessions were particularly challenging. On a number of occasions when the therapist arrived my father would quip, *"This would be a good time for a heart attack."* Since there was a steady stream of different personnel he was able to use his quip a number of times. Nonetheless he consistently cooperated and often ended up doing more than he thought he could. When each session ended he never failed to graciously thank the therapists for their patience with him.

Days and nights in the nursing facility were bleak and timeless. It was depressing when company was present so we could only imagine how Dad felt when he was alone. More than once he used the word *agony* and referred to himself as, *"a prisoner being tortured every day."* Neither did he seem to entertain a lot of hope for having a better quality of life in the near future. For example, what the medical professionals described as efforts to walk, Dad pronounced as, *"being dragged across the floor."* And during the visit of one of his granddaughters, he casually interjected into a conversation how irritating he found it to often be sitting in poop.

* * *

Leaving after my visit to return to my obligations in Williamsburg was difficult, but during my time at my parents' home a long-time resident of mine had died and I needed to get back to officiate at the funeral later than week. The tug of war between being there for my family and being there for my "parishioners" seemed like an ever-present tension, but if there was anyone who could relate to this dilemma, it was my dad.

Getting Dad situated in the nursing facility was a milestone, but we were well aware that his Medicare Rehabilitation benefits were limited and we needed to think about the next phase of this dizzying nightmare. Carol, candidate for canonization, had committed to remain with our parents a third month, until April 1st, which was over a month away, but time was quickly passing.

Marilee and Donna, who hadn't been as involved, were dealing with major challenges health and family-wise. Rather than being critical of what part anyone was playing, our sibling policy consisted of two parts: gratitude for anything anyone was able to do or contribute, and collaboration without judgment. Coverage had rotated smoothly and was generally assumed by a sister who could clear her schedule as the need arose. Up to this time a natural evolution of who would step up to the plate kept the ball rolling. And, amazingly at no time during this whole event did I ever hear any sister criticize the lack of participation of any other sister. We all just pooled the resources we had and were grateful that up to that point my parents were adequately supported.

Ironically this method of teamwork was somewhat in contrast to how my sisters and I operated in our childhood. My mother - obviously – had spent quite a few years of our childhood pregnant. Unluckily she was not a picture of health during these pregnancies, particularly in their early months. Thus during those occasions of illness, she delegated the household chores to those of us capable enough to do them, with the caveat that she did not care who did what, just that it got done and without fighting. For weeks at a time, she pretty much lived in her upstairs bedroom and left us to it.

Our solution to managing all the responsibilities was an actual written document, a rather rigid constitution, that not only stipulated the guidelines for who was responsible for what duties but also incorporated penalties when someone did not fulfill an assignment. Somehow word of our document got out in the community, and in the March 3rd, 1965 Rockland County Journal News there was a picture of the seven of us dressed in our Sunday finest, sedately sitting and smiling at one another. Its headline read *"Seven Is The Lucky Number At Rev. Flynn's 'Girl's Town'"*.

Here are some excerpts from the accompanying article: *The Flynn Girls have a "constitution" which they drew up themselves, complete with systems for all kinds of chores. The dishwashing system is intricate enough to even cover company and emergencies. Problem spots such as what's watched on the TV and who answers the telephone are dealt with. In case a new problem arises, they simply write it down, give opinions and amend the constitution....... Borrowing of clothes is not permitted unless there is a mutual agreement. The constitution stipulates a 25 cent fine is charged for each day an illegal borrower uses an outfit.....*"

This constitution remained in effect for quite a few years. Apparently this document, based more on unbending justice than mercy, established the underpinnings for cooperation and collaboration that served us well during my parents' final years. But happily, over time we had grown more compassionate and less rigid in coping with the responsibilities thrust upon us. And though there were a lot of us, at one point in Dad's medical saga, one of my sisters commented, *"Seven is not enough."*

* * *

Meanwhile it was difficult to ascertain what was really transpiring with our dad. He was still extremely weak, and tired of being pushed, shoved, prodded and poked. Plus, he disliked the lack of control over his time, stated he felt tortured, and resisted making decisions for himself. A mini-mental test was administered as part of his medical protocol, and he scored almost a hundred percent. Sadly his clear mental status seemed to be exacerbating his unhappiness. Frequently, at all hours of the day or night, he'd call home frustrated because no one responded when he rang his bell for assistance. This of course was very stressful for my mother. On several occasions, when he was desperate, he'd call Linnea, who was eight hundred miles away in Chicago, and she in turn would call the nurses' desk down the hall from him to get assistance. This situation was agony for all of us.

During all this my mother soldiered on. She believed the presence of a family member with my dad was therapeutic and though it exhausted her, she herself spent four or five hours a day at the facility. My parents had always supported each other. They met at an Oratorio Contest the year my mom was a college sophomore and my dad, a senior. It was my mother who inspired my father to begin his writing career.

Now, my mother felt her role was to encourage Dad to eat. But not surprisingly, much of Dad's discomfort revolved around eating issues. Pureed food wasn't appetizing and typically eating caused him to feel nauseous and he would often vomit. Here's a snapshot of his eating dilemma.

Today Dad began to wax poetic about how he wished that instead of being where he was, he would rather be sitting down in Louie's or the Greenhouse Café, eating the way he used to and how it would be so nice to enjoy a good meal there. He also said, "Oh how I wish I could get out of my bed and walk into my kitchen and eat my morning egg." A moment later he began coughing lunch back up and he noticed that what he coughed up looked tinged with red and he remarked that that red drink was probably the culprit. At one point mom left the room to cry in the hall and I could really sympathize with her. It was just so sad to see him longing for simple abilities, which we take for granted, to walk into his own kitchen and cook and enjoy even something simple to eat." (Susan)

The purpose of Dad's stay in the nursing facility was for him to be rehabilitated to a level of functioning where it would be safe and feasible for him to return home. Medicare subsidizes this service if certain guidelines are met. Basically, there has to be a qualified hospitalization and the patient has to be capable of benefiting from the therapy. When he was discharged from the hospital, my dad could do little more than sit up for a brief time, so the consensus was, with physical, occupational and speech (swallow) therapy, progress towards more independence was foreseeable.

Almost two months post surgery we all wondered if any headway was being made or to what level of independence my father could be rehabilitated. One of my sister's observed, *"Dad seems so tired and weak. It is hard to know what is really best for him. What is the line between potential beneficial rehab and torture? As we were walking together, I knew mom and I were on the same wavelength when she said, "Well, at least we're giving him a chance."*

A requirement of Medicare was that patients in a facility have periodic Care-Plan meetings with the treatment team. Our father's initial one was scheduled during his second week and Linnea had volunteered to be present for it. We were all hoping that a discussion of the involved parties would shed more light on current status and what the future held.

* * *

All of us were amazed at how gracious our father continued to be to the staff and those he interacted with. He had expressed the desire not to have visitors other than family but getting people to honor those wishes was challenging. One afternoon, when he really needed to rest after a morning of therapy, a stream of visitors stopped by.

A man Dad mentored one night a week for several years stopped in. Poor dad really needed to rest but again, he was so gracious. The man walked in and Dad said, "I have some fond memories of time spent with you." I started to tear up and I saw tears in that man's eyes at a few points. They visited for a while and Dad said, "I feel some diarrhea coming out and there's not a thing I can do about it!" I almost burst out laughing. That poor man had no idea what to say to that. Good old Dad knows how to clear out a room!

After that visit Mom called the church (that Dad had served for 40 years) *and they put an announcement in the bulletin that said, "Thank you for your cards and notes. They mean much at this time given that Pastor Flynn cannot have any visitors.* (Susan)

* * *

Knowing if, when, and how long to visit a patient is an art one masters with experience. Factors such as your relationship to the person, the person's medical condition, their preferences, and their status play a part. There are individuals who prefer (often for good reason) not to have visitors, and if that wish is made known, it should be respected.

A popular resident in my convalescent center, who was under Hospice care, even with a sign on his door stating "No Visitors", was inundated with guests, who apparently felt the sign did not apply to them. In large healthcare facilities it is almost impossible to prohibit visitors for specific individuals. The solution for this resident and his family was to physically relocate to the local Hospice House, where a *no visitor policy* could be enforced so that this gentleman could be in the peaceful environment he needed for a good death.

* * *

When Linnea arrived her assessment was that Dad's physical condition had definitely improved during the three weeks since she'd seen him. She also talked to Dad's doctor who agreed and expressed optimism regarding his recovery. Dad's surgeon also paid a visit and instructed Dad (as he'd done numerous times before) he needed to do two things: exercise and eat food. He told Dad to think of food as medicine and if he regurgitated it, to just try again. (Easy to advocate if you aren't the patient.)

Before March ended, Dad received word that the book he had submitted just before he was initially hospitalized-- his forty-third - had been accepted for publication. When Mom brought him the letter his initial response was, *"My last book!"* and then he sort of edited himself and said, *"Well, now I've finished everything I've started. Every manuscript I've ever sent in for publication has been accepted."*

Much to everyone's surprise Dad chose to be present at the Care Plan meeting. It yielded some insight into where things were and communicated progress observed. The therapists estimated it would take approximately four more weeks for Dad to gain strength and improve his ability enough to do his *Activities of Daily Living*, a recognized classification health professionals utilize to determine a patient's functioning level. These activities, referred to as ADL's, include ambulating, transferring, grooming, bathing, dressing, eating and toileting. The team praised Dad for the progress he had made, which inspired him to focus on what he had accomplished rather than what he was unable to do.

Despite this, and despite the encouraging information shared, no one yet knew what realistic hope there was for the future. Would Dad ever get back to a quality of life that he truly found gratifying because he certainly was not finding meaning or pleasure in his current day-to-day existence? He still had major continence issues; Carol commented that his frequent poops were enough to make a skunk faint. Food he commented, had no sense of taste and felt like glue in his stomach; and at night he wished it were daytime, and during daytime, he wished it were night.

* * *

The lack of responsiveness by the facility staff continued to be an issue particularly after visitors had gone home. One night Dad was in pain for an extended time; he tossed and turned but could not rouse any help and finally at 5:00 a.m. called Mom who in turn called the nurses' desk. Apparently his pain was from a kink in his catheter that had caused a back up. The next day he ruefully quipped that he did not need therapy that day, because the thrashing about he'd been engaged in all night had served as sufficient exercise.

In her emails, Carol often facetiously referred to her surroundings as *"Narnia,"* and to Dad as *"Jack"* (as in a box) whose wellbeing seems to either be up or down. Though my mother continued to push him, other family members began to question how to best help Dad– coerce him to eat and be more active, insist on therapy, or let him be, and not make demands on him. And we all wondered how much his efforts actually impacted the outcome? Were the feeding tube and his little bit of eating by mouth really giving him strength? Was he actually absorbing nutrition? Was his discouragement depression or acknowledgement that his life was coming to an end? Were we overstepping the line from encouragement to coercion regarding his exercise and eating efforts?

At the beginning of his nursing home stay, Dad told me that he felt like he was in a pit fifteen to twenty feet below the ground, from which he could not escape. He wanted to know what he could hope for. I responded that we were all hoping he would get strong enough to take care of himself, to go home, sit in his chair, eat, when he wanted and get back to writing.

He said he was not sure that could happen and kept repeating that he was an 87-year-old man. Then I asked him if it would it make things better if he didn't feel pressured to exercise and eat and - with a lot of feeling - he responded, *"Oh, that would be wonderful."* But he also added that he knew my mother was very worried about how things were going.

I was hoping, in a new environment, a change from the hospital, that dad might improve. However, after a month in the rehab program with little progress, I couldn't help wondering if what was happening here was sanctioned persecution. His surgeon, the aids, the therapists and my mother were engaged in a two-fold mission - to have him ingest food one way or another and to have him exert himself physically. However, no matter how much he could make himself eat and even with the assistance of the feeding tube, he still was weak. After receiving therapy for a month he showed little improvement. The attention paid to numbers, like the level of his albumen, deflected attending to the evidence of his realistic state: he was exhausted, incontinent and eating resulted in more discomfort than pleasure. Living was torture and he was not finding it meaningful or enjoyable.

I had observed numerous patients in the rehab facility where I worked. Many arrived from a scheduled surgery- such as a joint replacement - and for these individuals, rehab was a godsend; it was the means to resume the life they had previously been living. Others arrived after unforeseen events like a stroke, debilitation from illness or a fall. After several weeks these individuals either continued to demonstrate progress, eventually reached a plateau and were discharged to home or a long-term nursing facility.

Occasionally patients were admitted and it was obvious from the get-go that even though they met the guidelines for Medicare rehab, there was no way it was going to happen. They were dying, and in those instances the healthcare team, the medical director, nurses, social worker and I helped them transition to Hospice care; many returning home or elsewhere to live out their final days. The reality was no one really knew, or was willing to admit it, if my father's rehabilitation was futile or beneficial.

Unfortunately, if his lack of progress no longer demonstrated that there was benefit in the therapy, Medicare funds would no longer cover his stay at the facility. One of the things we all agreed on was that we did not want to pay privately for him to remain in a facility we could not trust to provide adequate care. Thus, the tempestuous journey continued.

Not long after the care plan meeting, on a Thursday evening, his feeding tube malfunctioned and Dad was told he'd have to return to the hospital to have it re-inserted, but it could not happen for a couple of days, because of the weekend. Before the hospital visit was scheduled, the surgeon visited Dad and told him that the additional nutrition from a feeding tube was beneficial to him. (Actually there was no evidence or indication this was true.) So, because the feedings were done during the night and Dad did not find having the tube particularly inconvenient, he acceded to the surgeon's advice.

Linnea also had a conversation with Dad, assessing his desire for the tube's reinsertion. He told her that both the medical director at the facility and his surgeon told him how great it would be if it did not need to be reinserted since he was eating more, but because he could not promise them he would be able to eat enough by mouth to get his nutritional needs met, it was decided: the tube would be reinserted. Sadly no one acknowledged that even with the feeding tube, there was no guarantee he would receive the nourishment he required.

As a healthcare chaplain I believe the physician should have honestly acknowledged that after two months - even with the feeding tube - my father was not getting adequate nutrition. This also would have been an opportune time for the physician to find out if my father would consider it a life with quality if he required a feeding tube for the remainder of his life.

During my years in healthcare chaplaincy I had developed faith in patients' capacity - those who were mentally healthy - to be able to discern what was best for them. I believe if there had been someone available for my dad - a social worker, other medical professional, or a chaplain - who was a gifted listener and who offered a safe space, that possibly he could have found a means to share his own intuition: that he was never going to get back to an acceptable level of independence. My father, unfortunately, was up against his surgeon and the medical director, who both were unwilling to acknowledge that he wasn't improving, and who measured success by delaying death. I believe it's the duty of physicians to share the reality with patients and families when there is little reason to believe full recovery is a possibility.

A week after his feeding tube had malfunctioned Dad, in a very weakened state, went to the hospital for an outpatient procedure and successfully had the feeding tube reinserted. However, as Dad himself observed, he had made negligible progress. He was weak, shaky and unenthusiastic about most everything.

Furthermore, Carol was several weeks away from having to return to her family and teaching position in South Dakota. Thus, we communally were realizing that patchwork coverage was not going to be sufficient care for the needs of our parents. Who knew how long it would be before Dad could do anything for himself and with a wife unable to walk it was apparent extra support was needed. My sisters and I had to perceive their situation as chronic rather than transitory; realistically acknowledging it could go on for months or years. One of my sisters referred to the circumstances as being *"inconvenient,"* recognizing what an appalling and misguided understatement that truly was for each one of us.

* * *

Providing some respite for Carol was crucial to sustaining her for her final weeks as caregiver. Knowing this, I made arrangements for a long weekend trip to New York.

The facility Dad resided in had an unwelcoming atmosphere. The actual doorway was like walking into the entrance of an old house. A caged receptionist sat at the desk and seldom greeted visitors. Inside the door was a makeshift area that served as a beauty parlor. Extending in two directions from it were hallways, typically with residents slumped over in wheelchairs in the doorways of their rooms.

Hospitals and nursing facilities are not places elders want to live out their lives, but our society has not yet come up with viable alternatives. In an effort to better emulate a home-like environment, there is a movement to shift the focus in nursing facilities to patient or person-centered care. In a person-centered environment, in an attempt to emulate being at home, individuals decide what time they want to awaken, be dressed, eat and bathe, rather than accommodating themselves to a schedule established by the institution. Physically the more progressive centers are replacing traditional hallway floor plans with neighborhood complexes, open floor plans where a combination kitchen and living area are the hub with individual resident rooms on the peripheral. Rather than differentiating tasks of house cleaners, dining servers, etc. each staff member pitches in with a variety of chores emulating a family caregiver. Unfortunately, my father did not have the benefit of this type of environment, an environment that is more amenable to the spirits of people whose circumstances are bleak.

* * *

Dad seemed somewhat perkier to me when I arrived at his room, located at the end of the hallway. We talked for a while about my husband and son. I told him about the wonderful new and serious girlfriend my son was dating. The downside to the relationship was that it was long distance because my son lived in Las Vegas and his girlfriend resided in New York City. The upside was the two of them could visit my dad when my son traveled to New York.

I asked my dad what would help during this time, and he mentioned that he really missed taking his daily naps. Often he was in the wheelchair and couldn't get anyone to put him to bed when he got sleepy. For over sixty years he had been taking a ten-minute power nap after lunch and he really suffered when he couldn't.

So we brought his favorite chair, a recliner he traditionally took naps in, to the facility. Carol and I were able to get it into her vehicle and then carry it through the building, to Dad's room.

Luckily the arrival of the recliner was well received by Dad. In the coming weeks he utilized the familiar chair many days to get his nap and found it much more comfortable than the wheelchair for watching television. I am not sure having his recliner made him stronger, but it certainly helped him tolerate his situation. It seems that people who have spent little or no time as a patient can't appreciate how modest gestures and conveniences have the capacity to make big differences in quality of life.

Like many bed-bound patients it was important that my father have amenities like his telephone, a glass of water, the TV remote, and his call bell within reach.

However, frequently aids or nurses would do their assigned task, and then walk out of the room without returning the over-the-bed table within reach, where the items were. At times patients need a pillow repositioned or a blanket added. For anyone who works in or visits in healthcare facilities, a helpful way to end a visit is to ask, *"Is there anything I can do for you before I go?"* Not only does this demonstrate a caring attitude, but often a small deed that is requested will bring the patient added reassurance or comfort. And it may preclude the patient from ringing his call bell as frequently.

* * *

A typical day for me when I was at my parents' house began with an early morning run, an enjoyable beginning to the day. Then, being the only coffee drinker in the family, on my way home, I'd purchase a cup of coffee. By the time I arrived back at my parents' house, my mother had finished her morning routine preparing for the day. She always dressed fashionably, even on the infrequent days she didn't plan to leave the house. I'd shower, pull on blue jeans and a t-shirt, make a lunch for us, then we'd be off to the nursing home.

I never knew what to expect when I arrived. Some days Dad was still in bed, hadn't been cleaned up, and other days he was already in physical therapy. Though having no schedule was a minor inconvenience to me, it was frustrating to my very organized father; having his life at the beck and call of the staff, with little interesting diversions.

The nursing facility had an Activities Director but my erudite, book-writing dad did not find Bingo or group sings very fulfilling. The majority of residents, in the section where he resided, had memory issues. Thus, he pretty much kept to himself and relied on family for companionship.

My mother and I ate with him somewhere other than his room. We typically found an area with privacy. My father's enthusiasm for meals was still nonexistent so my mother often spent the meal cajoling him to just have a few more bites. Sometimes he was nauseous and other times he regurgitated the food. Little of the day was pleasant, but meals were the most tension-filled.

I felt profound sadness for my dad, compassion for my mom, and admiration for Carol for her fortitude. As my relatively short visit approached its end, I was chomping at the bit to return home to my husband and my regular life, which, when I compared my lot to my dad's, brought on guilt feelings.

* * *

When I returned home it was the middle of March, and my father had been institutionalized close to three months. Though spring's arrival in Virginia comes sooner than it does in New York, I was not feeling the effects of its beauty and rebirth that year. I was sad and realized that I was experiencing anticipatory grief, a reaction that precedes an impending loss, that often can be isolating because it's not understood by others. It was not clear to me exactly what my loss would be, but I sensed one coming.

April 1st, Carol's date to leave was approaching when she sent out the following: *Wow what a day!!!! I will not go into detail, as Mom will every chance she gets! She is on the phone now with her third replay already!!! When dad was doing his therapy walk he collapsed, slowly going down on his knees. We got him into a wheelchair and they started yelling 'help' and people came running. Dad's eyes were rolling and he was gasping for air. They got him to his room and could not find a pulse; they were talking about his Do Not Resuscitate order and the head nurse started ordering people out of the room. It was not something I ever want to experience again but at the time nothing would have made me leave that room! He got white as a sheet and his body was clammy and very very cold. They got him stabilized without having to attempt resuscitation and the decision to take him to the hospital was made by Mom. They did numerous tests and think that he had a blood clot move from his leg to his lungs. He will be in the hospital until Monday at least. He has an infected tube and other things but honestly I was so exhausted by 6pm when Dr. C was briefing us that I don't want to give you false info. Mom is exhausted and edgy and I mirror that, so I will go hibernate upstairs. Love you all, wish you were here!*

My journal entry resulting from this news was: *When I arrived home from officiating at two funerals, an email was waiting from Carol. Dad had collapsed, clammy breathless, etc. He was stabilized and then transported to the hospital. Apparently he had a blood clot go to his lung and he also has an infection in a tube. Must've been traumatizing for Mom and Carol. Gene's* (my husband's) *response was this was exactly what you were afraid would happen. If it's all a nightmare for us hearing about it, it must be unimaginable for Dad. I don't want Dad to die but I don't want him to live like this.*

Dad ended up recuperating in the hospital for over a week. Unfortunately he somehow developed the idea that this blood clot incident was the result of relentless therapists coercing him to walk. The ironic spin on these unfortunate events was that Medicare could justify extending his benefits in the nursing facility. His weeklong hospitalization in effect allowed him additional time in rehab, which he needed, since it also set him back strength-wise.

Interestingly, he had relished his hospitalization. The environment was peaceful, he got great care and personnel did not badger him to exercise and eat. His day nurse, coincidentally a long-time parishioner, seemed happy attending to his every need. Consequently, when discharge time came, he lacked enthusiasm for returning to the nursing facility.

Apparently, a result of his near-death experience was he was left somewhat confused. For the previous six weeks a word he used incessantly was *"nauseated,"* and now he seemed unable to remember it. One of my sisters made the comment that truer words had never been spoken when Carol had weeks earlier dubbed Dad "Jack-in-the-Box."

* * *

Spring, April and Easter arrived, and Carol knew she'd be returning, with mixed feelings, to her life as mother and teacher in South Dakota. Meanwhile in the face of her leaving, Linnea and Susan took the initiative in organizing support services so Mom could not only be safe home alone, but also have transportation to the facility. For both my parents' sake these visits needed to continue as frequently as possible.

It was unusual for Dad to directly talk about his unhappiness with his surroundings, and he never discussed returning home, maybe because he was unsure it would ever become a reality. One afternoon when a sister was visiting with her children they were all sitting around dreaming what they would buy if they had a lot of money. When it was my father's turn, he thought for a moment and then said, *"I'd dynamite this place."* My sister then asked,

"With you in it?" and he responded, *"I'd be at one end and I'd dynamite the other."*

My father must've been extremely discouraged. After over three months of aggressive treatment and institutional medical care he was unable to do much of anything for himself. Being an intelligent and rational human being he had to have questioned if recovery were possible. But, because no one could or would definitively state that his condition would not improve, the sanctioned persecution continued.

The day Carol had to leave to return to South Dakota, she saw our mother weeping as they were leaving the facility. My mother explained to her that when she was saying her goodbyes to Dad, he apologized to her for not writing my mother a holiday Easter missive, a tradition he had maintained for several decades on Valentine's Day, Easter, Mother's Day, their wedding anniversary and her birthday. My mother was touched that he had even considered writing one that year, but was sad both that he was unable to do so, and that she might never receive another one.

Often, these missives were four pages of single-spaced typewritten print and they all pretty much reiterated his feelings about his gratitude in being her husband. They normally included a description of her vivaciousness, joy, beauty, warmth, and her parental dedication to the seven of us. Many incorporated his wit like his mentioning in the

60th anniversary letter how they attained this *milestone*, which definitely was not a *millstone*. And he never failed to mention how little she'd changed since they met when she was a beautiful college sophomore.

* * *

After Carol's departure my mom was home alone. Though she eagerly anticipated visits when any of her daughters could make them, she seemed content to be by herself. Her mental attitude and safety awareness were impressive which reassured us all that she could cope with her daily activities and the demands of life despite being wheelchair bound.

Undoubtedly the uncertainty about Dad's future was taking its toll on all of us, but particularly on Mom. Dad was losing weight and his weakness caused him to dread his physical therapy sessions. With my nurse sister's intervention the schedule of feeding was revised so that Dad might be hungrier when his meals arrived. However, he continued to want to be put to bed after his afternoon therapy sessions where he was content to remain until the next morning.

When my sister was visiting for Mother's Day, the surgeon dropped by to see Dad and offered him the opportunity to have chemo or radiation therapy. The surgeon's point was that after this type of surgery there is always a chance the tumor will reoccur, so having one of these therapies would be reassurance. He said the radiation would be more invasive than the chemo, but that chemo was very debilitating. He said he was required to present Dad with these choices but his advice was not to do either of them. My father asked the surgeon his thoughts on hospice and the surgeon's response was, *"Absolutely not."* He then informed my dad that he was not ready for hospice because, he said, *"You are getting better and we all expect you to go home soon."*

Having spent fifteen years as a Hospice Chaplain I realized that an ill person taking the initiative to question their appropriateness for Hospice is not only uncommon but an appeal for understanding, for an opportunity to acknowledge what's going on. Sadly, when my dad attempted to open this door, it was slammed in his face. Although he may have sensed that he wasn't recovering, he wasn't granted a hearing for his feelings and thoughts.

Many people, including medical professionals, prior to experiencing Hospice Care personally, do not realize that often having Hospice services improves quality of life and in some cases, actually extends life. And more often than not, recipients of Hospice services state they wish they'd called in Hospice earlier. It has also been my experience that seriously ill individuals sense, at some level, when they are dying, and are on a trajectory that doesn't include recovery.

I have to wonder how my father's suffering could have been mitigated had the door to comfort care been opened at this time, rather than the regime he faced: being forced to do therapy and being pressured to ingest food.

Hospice, under Medicare, has strict guidelines for admission and if a patient meets the criteria - which I am confident my dad would have at that point - I feel it should be the patient's decision to forego aggressive care and focus on comfort. Shifting the focus sooner rather than later, to quality of life for the remaining time, I believe would have helped my father's ending be more satisfying.

Typically when a family is embroiled in the middle of such tumult, as our family was, it chooses passivity, (as we did) acceding to the medical experts in charge, about how to proceed. However, I don't believe that's the way it will continue in the future. For one thing, more doctors are becoming aware - both because of the high cost of futile medical intervention at the end of life and because they are more educated about the advantages of comfort care, that extending someone's life indefinitely - particularly if they are frail and elderly - can be doing harm, a violation of the Hippocratic oath. Additionally, as baby boomer children share their parents' gruesome and prolonged dying experiences, they are learning there are alternatives such as palliative care, if requested.

* * *

After the surgeon left, my sister and mother tried to query Dad regarding his feelings of pursuing cancer treatments, but he showed greater interest in getting back into the bed than discussing his future. His reaction, to me, seems understandable. Not only was he probably physically spent, but his plea to have someone acknowledge his feelings had been ignored and all he had left to expect was more of the same frustrations.

And, as one of my sisters summed it up, *"The whole thing is worse than anyone could imagine."*

Coming Home

Even though there had been rumblings that Dad's discharge would be coming soon, the announcement that Medicare would no longer pay for his nursing home stay was announced with less than a week's notice. Thus, Dad's discharge day, after his four month stay, was set for the following Thursday and my sister Donna and I hurriedly arranged to come to the parsonage to be the transition team and take the first caregiving shift.

On Tuesday and Wednesday Home Care services delivered a hospital bed, a commode, a wheelchair and a feeding pump, a device we had been told we'd be trained to operate prior to discharge. (The training never occurred.) Neither had anyone in our family been educated about diabetic maintenance, which now was much more complicated because my father was insulin-dependent. The medication list that was provided upon discharge, we discovered, included every drug my dad had been on during his entire nursing home stay, and was not narrowed down to the medications he currently was taking. It wasn't until we were home that we realized from the discharge orders that there was no way to differentiate between Dad's current prescriptions and his cumulative past prescriptions, a precarious situation to address.

When someone resides in a total care facility, hospital supplies like gloves, adult diapers, bed protectors, and gowns are available as needed. My sister and I were rather clueless both in knowing what supplies would be needed and where to acquire them. Unfortunately, Nurse Linnea wasn't available to assist us because she had a professional commitment in Korea.

In my professional experience with Hospice I'd observed countless situations where patients are cared for in their homes with the help of home health services or hospice care. These patients ran the gamut from being mostly self-sufficient to those who were bed-bound and required total care. The caregiver circumstances also varied from the availability of numerous family members, paid professional teams, to a solitary spouse or child shouldering almost all of the responsibility of day-to-day care. However, it wasn't until my sister, Donna, and I found ourselves in our childhood home with a mother in a wheelchair who was accustomed to being in charge (her nickname, Mother General was undisputedly earned) and a father who was clueless about his diabetic and prescription regime and barely capable of transferring from bed, to chair, to toilet, that my admiration for the caregivers I had observed over the years became heartfelt.

Though both my sister and I were medical novices, we had to maintain a façade of control in order to gain the confidence of our parents. One thing I learned from those days is that we need one another to get by in this world. If I didn't have a sister to stand and commiserate with as we adjusted to caring for Dad at home, I don't believe I could have remained standing. We also made a pact that we wouldn't share how awful the situation was with our other sisters, because we didn't want to scare them needlessly. And, we were hoping that in a few days the situation would be in better shape, if we didn't inadvertently kill our Dad beforehand.

Recognizing that we lacked basic knowledge and expertise we asked a family friend, whose spouse was diabetic, to come to the house and train us how to handle my Dad's diabetes. Our persistence in alerting the doctor's office to the seriousness of the prescription dilemma got the issue resolved before the weekend. And, fortuitously one of my dad's former parishioners was a home-care nurse who offered her services.

Our parents' home, the parsonage, was built in the early 1900's and though it had a half bath on the first floor, all five bedrooms were on the second floor. When my mother became wheelchair bound eight years earlier, she turned the playroom, a room with a sliding door adjacent to the dining room, into her bedroom. To further accommodate her, a toilet was eventually installed in the back pantry area and a handicapped shower installed where the washer had been. Except for her recovery times after shoulder surgeries, these served her adequately.

Because a quiet space and privacy were necessities for my dad, my mother decided to give him her bedroom, the playroom. She moved into the adjacent room, the dining room, which unfortunately was also the passage to the kitchen, and a room that could not be closed off. Other than the kitchen and foyer, the other downstairs room was the living room, which was separated from the dining room by the foyer. It was hardly an ideal situation - there was a lack of privacy – the toilet was a long distance from the living room and playroom, but it was what was available and for them, it was home sweet home.

* * *

My sister and I, and the sisters who followed on our heels, navigated those first weeks of caring for Dad at home, but we were so busy and exhausted that few reports were written. A major problem we all experienced was my father's inability to get to the toilet in time. As had been the case since the feeding tube insertion, Dad suffered from frequent bouts of diarrhea. On some occasions he could make it to the bathroom in time, but often he didn't. And because he wasn't getting sufficient nutrition, he was weak and it became increasingly difficult for him to walk much at all, so we needed to ration his trips. He enjoyed watching television in the living room. Our solution, which he resigned to with apathy, was to utilize adult diapers.

On Sunday morning, Father's Day, he was so weak from frequent trips to the bathroom that when he required a change of diapers, we did not know how we would get him from the living room to his bed, to make the change. Our living room was right off the hallway of the front door and his bed was across the house. My sister and I were totally relieved when the home care nurse -the parishioner who'd offered to help us - showed up after church while we were pondering our dilemma.

We described our problem and the nurse suggested, though there was little privacy, that since there were three of us, we could change him while he stood up in the living room. Two of us supported him and my sister did the diapering. It was messy, challenging and took a lot of effort on all our parts. That first time, when we thought we were done, the doorbell rang and simultaneously we discovered the diaper was on the wrong way. At our wits end, the three of us burst out laughing. My poor father seemed desensitized to the situation and I can remember thinking it would have been difficult to think up or stage the fiasco we'd just lived through.

Things improved somewhat the next day when the Home Care Nurse who was responsible for Dad's care plan made her initial visit and scheduled an aid to come in a couple of times a week to help with bathing and other nursing tasks. The nurse also helped us with Dad's feeding tube situation and eventually those who needed to know, were trained how to feed him. We also found a store that sold medical supplies and purchased what experience taught us we needed.

* * *

Throughout the next weeks several other sisters took turns at the parsonage. The Medicare home health agency provided an aid that came mornings for several hours and evenings for a brief time to prepare Dad for bed. After Dad had been home for about ten days, as June was ending, one sister reported, *"Dad is very weak and frail. He seems to be worse than I remember him being the last few times I visited him at the facility. There does not seem to be a moment of the day or night during which he is not nauseous. He sleeps off and on all day in his recliner and isn't very interested in TV."*

Throughout this time we all were plagued as one of my sisters described it, *by an underlying anxiety,* because we knew the current plan of care, where we took turns being our parents constant companions, was not sustainable. However, after two weeks at home, a daily routine was established and things settled down. But, Dad's extreme weakness continued, he slept much of the day and was restless at night.

My sisters and I are educated, capable, resourceful human beings, but this cobbled-together, long-distance caregiving gig was a much bigger challenge for us than most of what life dealt us in the past. Additionally, not knowing how long the situation would persist; we realized we needed outside resources. One of the individuals whom Mom had hired to transport her to and from the nursing home, who had some nursing experience and was caring, competent and reliable offered to take responsibility for Dad's feeding tube and insulin testing both morning and nights. Teresa, or St. Teresa, as she came to be known to the sisters, was just what the doctor ordered and more importantly, someone who was not only competent and reliable, but a person our dad really trusted. And, she lived just up the street.

In addition, Linnea arranged the services of a full-time companion who would actually live with our parents, and care for our Dad, with the help of our St. Teresa. When Donna, the sister who had shared the homecoming experience with me, heard the news this was part of her response. *"I've got to tell you. I've been losing sleep over this whole situation. I am totally wiped out from my little stint there and honestly don't know when I could handle doing anything like that ever again.*

* * *

Although my parents' finances were in good order, none of us were privy to the specifics of their resources. Though Dad had spent forty years a minister at a large church, he was never one to ask much for himself. He and my mother had always resided in the parsonage; and it was the church's "gift of its use" to live in after his retirement. Apparently though, combining the money they saved from having subsidized housing, with the revenue from his books and an inheritance from mom's parents, there were funds, at least for the present, to cover his care.

A stipulation of the agreement with the home-health service organization, which was the source of the live-in aid, was the caregiving responsibilities would not include my mother's care. None of us saw this as an issue because she had been coping well on her own since Carol returned to South Dakota, two months previously.

After making all these arrangements and actually initiating a schedule of care for the glucose testing and feeding tube with Teresa, before she left, because of Dad's querying the surgeon about Hospice, Linnea had a conversation with Dad and asked him if he ever felt like life was not worth living this way. He told her it was hard to describe to someone who had energy, how much discomfort there is in sustained extreme weakness. He admitted how difficult eating was with the persistent nausea and talked about the indignities of incontinence. He questioned if the feeding tube was keeping him alive and if it would be immoral to have it removed. My sister assured him that he would be refusing extreme life sustaining measures, not committing suicide, should he make that choice. He then wondered if that choice would devastate my mother and Linnea told him that she believed

Mom would agree with any decision he made because she loved him and saw how much he was suffering.

Linnea suggested he talk with me about this because as a healthcare chaplain, I had experience with people stopping use of their feeding tubes. He thought this was a good idea but said he'd wait till I visited because talking on the phone would be difficult. Though my sister matter-of-factly reported this painful discussion, it took its toll on her emotionally.

Fortuitously my husband and I were planning a quick visit to our parents the following weekend. And with the continued reports of my Dad's condition - sleeping much of the time, little interest in visits even from family members, and continued weakness - symptoms that often precede dying - it seemed like it couldn't happen soon enough.

* * *

The live-in aid for my dad was scheduled to be on-site in two days. Marilee, who was taking a shift, and who among the seven of us was the most artistic and domestic, had collected furniture and accessories from the various bedrooms and created a living space for the aid upstairs. Marilee also had installed a remote bell that my dad could ring to summon her services.

Annilee articulated our collective and continued gratitude for whatever each sister contributed: *I have to say that I have wonderful sisters. Carol was there for dad and mom through the months of dad's initial recovery. Janna, Donna and Susan came through BIG TIME by living through the chaos that existed after dad first came from the nursing home. And then Linnea has been so great in handling the medical issues, getting help and organizing things in Nanuet. Not to mention how amazing she was in talking to Dad about difficult subjects in a straightforward, sensitive way. And, Marilee did a masterful job of getting the guest room ready for the aid. I just feel so lucky to have all of you as my sisters!*

Annilee, the lawyer, asked our mother about her feelings regarding engaging the services of an attorney to protect the assets she had. Mom thought it was a good idea, and after my sister researched attorney friends and colleagues, she found a local estate lawyer willing to make a house call.

Meanwhile, Juliette, the live-in aid had arrived. Our father continued showing little interest in life and we were worried how our mother would fare with a stranger in her house. Her initial reaction was gratitude that Juliette could speak English! Mom realized intellectually that the live-in was going to replace having a daughter with her, but we knew time would tell how this would play out. Our St. Teresa, who by this time both our parents had come to love, continued to handle Dad's glucose checks and feeding tube on a daily and was on an on-call basis, plus home health continued some support and Juliette ideally was to manage the remainder. All of us planned to visit as frequently as we were able, but no longer to remain for extended time periods.

Linnea reported that after three weeks of at home, Dad was not doing well. His nauseous condition existed most of the time, he slept a lot and he'd developed a sore on his bottom. He was taking in very little nutrition, withdrawing more and had less tolerance for noise; evidence that he was failing to thrive. Conversely Dad's physician, getting his info mainly second hand from lab results, believed Dad was gradually improving. However none of us believed his quality of life was acceptable.

In early July when Dad's physician (not his surgeon) made a house call, his assessment changed. During the visit Dad asked him if he could engage the services of Hospice. The doctor agreed to his request, (which indicated he believed my father had six months or fewer to live), and wrote the order for Hospice Care. However, before the service could be put in place, Mom, in the face of excruciating back pain, had to be taken to the hospital by ambulance. Luckily, when this incident occurred, there was a daughter on site.

The hospital did not admit Mom but sent her home with painkillers determining that she'd suffered several compression fractures, some possibly from a previous injury. The Emergency Room doctor prescribed bed rest which meant Mom would be requiring a lot of personal assistance, including someone to give her a bedpan, etc. Now we were faced with two incapacitated people in the face of an agreement that Juliette's services were exclusive to my dad. Once again it appeared that a sister would have to be present until Mom became more independent.

Not surprisingly, Mother General was able to issue orders and run the show from her bed, which because of the bed's central location, revved up the stress level for everyone. To get to the kitchen or bathroom, one had to walk through her command post. Lacking physical facility, she seemed to feel the need to exert greater control over everything else, which was sometimes helpful and at other times not. Accordingly, she was able to preside over Dad's admission to in home Hospice Care.

When we engaged the services of Hospice, in mid-July, we found that their presence did not have much of an impact on Dad's caregiving situation, other than replacing the aid that was from the Home Care Agency with the aid from Hospice. However, it had great impact on peace of mind, knowing we could request assistance twenty four hours a day. The physician gave Dad a diagnosis of *failure to thrive,* and because Dad was already on a feeding tube when he was admitted, Hospice guidelines stated he would continue with it, unless he decided to ask that it be removed.

Part of the Hospice philosophy is to refrain from either prolonging or hastening death and removing the tube could hasten death for my father. However, had the tube not already been part of his treatment plan, inserting one might be construed as prolonging death. So typically patients under the care of a Hospice do not have feeding tubes unless they were present on admission. However, in end-of-life decision-making, the situation is seldom clear-cut and each case has to be evaluated on its own merit, taking into consideration varying opinions and instincts of family members, the patient, and medical professionals.

* * *

During her stay, Annilee witnessed Dad exhibiting some bizarre behavior. When he wasn't sleeping (which he did most of the time), he would just sit. When she tried to engage him in conversation, for example, by asking why he preferred one news station to another his reply was: *"That is just the sort of question I can't stand, because I can't think to answer it."* Dad also commented that he disliked bright lights and loud laughter.

When the EMT's had taken mom from the house, she said, *"Goodbye, Les"* and his response was a half-wave, while he stared straight ahead with open eyes. He also reported to Annilee that he didn't know if he could go on like this much longer. Then he mentioned to her that he thought he might be delusional because he saw a vision of Mom in a chair with beautiful flowing hair and when she tried to tell him something, she faded away. He also instructed Juliette, the aid, to not ignite any fires, which was peculiar because we did not have a working fireplace.

During her stay, hectic as it was, Annilee had been able to arrange a visit with an attorney who recommended that my parents resign as trustees of their trust, because of their compromised health. The attorney also underscored the urgency of getting it done while Dad was still deemed competent. So, Annilee put out the word to the sister alliance asking for volunteers to be primary trustees, volunteering to be one of them. She suggested that the sister who resides in New York be the other one, and Donna accepted. Thus, important matters were being attended to.

In addition to the confidence and trust all the sisters had in one another, we were fortunate to have parents who accepted the reality that a time comes when it is judicious to relinquish control over certain functions. My dad had done that with his driving. He recognized when his vertigo issues, that he'd tried unsuccessfully to have addressed medically, made him an unsafe driver, and though driving had been a huge aspect of a life of quality for him, he was willing to sacrifice it when he felt he was a danger to others. Thankfully, our family was spared the additional stress, ill will, and extended legal involvement, which often occur when parents refuse to abdicate their control over finances and other business at the prudent time.

* * *

Linnea was present when Elizabeth, the Hospice nurse, made her initial visit. She suggested as a comfort measure cutting back on Dad's night feeding, a suggestion that made him happy. When Linnea saw him early in the morning after this was instituted, he greeted her with the words, *"Happy Birthday."* She was amazed he'd even remembered, particularly since she herself had forgotten it was her fifty-ninth birthday.

A traditional quip we had heard from childhood from Dad on our birthdays was, *"You work like a horse and what do you get? Old."* Annilee included this quip in her birthday message to Linnea that read, *"Yes, you work like a horse and what do you get? Bedpans, medications, food tubes, hospice consultations, syringes and sleepless nights. Happy Birthday!!! What a way to spend your birthday!"*

Because our family members were so scattered and numerous, we sisters had long forsaken the tradition of exchanging birthday gifts with each other. Instead we initiated, at the time of our birthdays, the ritual of buying ourselves something we wanted and then communicated with gratitude to the rest of the sisters informing them what *"they'd"* bought us. The results were everyone got something they really wanted and there was no hassle buying and sending gifts to one another.

* * *

When I arrived for my weekend visit, I found my father not only weaker and thinner than my visit a month earlier, but also in a befuddled state. It was heartbreaking to see. Apparently he reacted quite dramatically to the medication Hospice prescribed for his nausea; he was reaching for imaginary stuff, talking to and about people that weren't there, wanting to drive and he was so restless he wouldn't sleep. He was actually so agitated Linnea, Juliette, and I took turns making sure he didn't climb out of his chair.

This was extremely disappointing to me because I had looked forward to having the discussion he was asking for regarding the removal of his feeding tube. It's one I wanted him to have but I had been reluctant to initiate because I was afraid either he or other family members would misconstrue it as me suggesting he stop using it.

Hospice is a wonderful service but after the official documents are signed and the team initially begins its service in your home, it brings numerous visitors and interruptions. Additionally, there are deliveries of equipment like hospital beds, commodes, oxygen, etc. Since my dad was switching from home health care to hospice care, all of the equipment, he was using had to be exchanged, along with the personnel from the home care service that were assisting him. Fortunately we still had the stability of Juliette's presence.

Making the change was a several daylong fiasco arranging who would come when, ensuring there would be no interruptions in service. This caused major upheaval in the household. My mother got so anxious she demanded Linnea put her on Dad's oxygen for a time. The mandate to exchange the providers for the hospital bed, oxygen, feeding tube and other durable health equipment is one of many examples of how insurance and regulations, rather than best practice, dictate patient care.

* * *

Because of my mother's medical issues, we'd returned to our sister-rotation routine. My personal opinion was that my dad was gradually moving to the end of life and coverage might not be necessary much longer.

Meanwhile my mother was evaluated to see if she was eligible for home care services. Because she needed help to bathe, toilet and transfer, and because she'd lost strength from inactivity she was deemed eligible and her physician prescribed services that included home health aids and physical therapy. Contrastingly, Dad was deteriorating; he was withdrawing into himself, was so weak he couldn't operate his recliner any more, he required assistance to transfer and stopped using his call bell to summon assistance.

Linnea sent out an emotional email saying, that when she said good-bye in mid July, that Dad told her how much he loved her and how much he appreciated all she'd done for him. She told him how much she loved him – and had a good cry on the way to the airport. She then told my mother she wasn't sure how much longer he'd live and suggested if the sisters wanted to speak with him, they should try to visit soon or call him on the phone, although he'd been significantly more passive the last few days.

I received her message with sadness and relief; sadness that Dad's life was coming to a close, and relief both that his ordeal would be over and that I was scheduled to be with him in the near future.

At this point in our email exchanges we began referring to our parents home as the *Parsonage Nursing Complex*. We had Hospice Services for Dad and Home Care Services for Mom.

A benefit of Hospice is that they provide many of the medical supplies, like gloves, pads, and feeding tube supplies, that we had previously been responsible for stocking, which alleviated the need for constant trips to the medical supply store in the next town. This was a great help to the person in charge. Additionally, they provide prescriptions related to the end-of-life diagnosis.

Caring for patients at home is not for the faint-of-heart. After experiencing, to the small extent I had caring for my father, I developed increased respect and admiration for all the Hospice family members I'd known in the past, who selflessly and tirelessly cared for dying loved ones in their homes, many for extended periods of time. Having the services of a Hospice is an immense benefit but it still leaves the majority of day-to-day and overnight caregiving to family members, paid staff and friends.

* * *

Susan and her family made a stop at the parsonage on their return home from their Vermont vacation. They arrived in the evening, which apparently had become the only time Dad seemed to demonstrate any awareness. He was able to greet them but his increased weakness and diminished alertness was obvious, even though only one week had passed since they'd visited. Accepting that Dad's life was coming to an end, Susan sent her family to a hotel and remained at the parsonage overnight, but sadly could not remain longer, leaving with the knowledge that probably she would not see her beloved father again.

There's no way to communicate the distress, the chaos, the uncertainty, the humor, etc. involved in all that transpires when a household is centered around illness and imminent death. Unexpected guests show up-- like a former husband with mental issues-- and strong emotions get expressed not necessarily in therapeutic ways. Laughter gets a little hysterical from lack of sleep and stress, tears come without warning and life seems to appear either more poignant and distinct or more dream-like depending on how one is feeling.

A couple of somewhat disconcerting incidents with our father occurred during this time, before my arrival. On one occasion Dad woke up in his recliner and asked Marilee if she had the death certificate. Marilee said, *"Whose death certificate?"* Dad said, *"I must not be dead yet,"* and he fell back asleep.

Another evening he woke up when he was being cleaned up by the aid and said, *"Call the doctor."* The aid gently questioned why and his response was *"I'm dead, call the doctor."* The aid got my mother to come, be with him and hold his hand and she asked him why he thought he was dead. He just responded that the doctor needed to pronounce him dead. Mom then prayed a lovely prayer and he got peaceful and when his granddaughter came in, he opened his eyes and smiled at her.

* * *

Dying is intense work. Much of the work goes on while the individual is in a dream-state and involves re-living or reviewing one's life, articulating what is needed for a peaceful death and resolving situations which were previously unresolved. In a dream-state, time is not perceived in the same fashion, as it is when one is alert. One often travels back in time remembering situations as if they were presently occurring. This can prove to be very disconcerting to family members, and confusing to the person who is dying.

I visited a dying resident a number of years ago who woke from a dream-like state and asked me what I was doing in Japan. He then saw his wife in the room and asked her the same question. What was probably occurring, was he was reliving his wartime experience in Japan, which was "real" to him, but he sensed there was something dissonant about our presence in his life at that time.

Many who have had a lot of experience working with dying patients believe that as one draws closer to death, the limits of time and space are lessened; one is not in the ordinary spatial and temporal consciousness. Perspective is more wide-ranging, time is fluid and there's a "thin" place between dream-like and reality awareness. Often patients near death carry on conversations with loved ones who have died and appear to be staring at someone or thing others in the room cannot envision.

A Hospice patient I worked with, got to the place where all he wanted was for his dying time to end. Therefore, each time he woke up from a nap or deep sleep he experienced disappointment that he was still alive. After this had been going on for several days I visited him and noticed a change; he seemed calmer. I mentioned to him that he seemed less restless and more at peace. He then told me he had woken up that morning with an incredible sense that all was well and he felt totally content and without a sense of time. It was like being held by a stillness within the flow of time. For him it was a wonderful feeling that he wished he could have enjoyed earlier in his living. It seemed like he was resting in the eternal now. This was an incredible gift to his family because he remained in this placid contented state until he lost consciousness and peacefully died a few days later.

Another feature of the dying process is the use of symbolic language. Some people might talk about getting dressed for a party, catching a plane, signing a death certificate or going home. Often these images are representative of preparation for death, and many times they bear a relationship to aspects of the dying person's life, incorporating their natural surroundings or former occupation. One former patient used to talk about having to finish milking the cows and another person had one more couch to upholster.

Also it is not uncommon for terminally ill patients to be ambivalent about death. One minute they might be making plans to attend a grandchild's graduation and the next they might be discussing their own funeral. I believe this is due in part to the inability of humans to imagine their own demise, or envisage a world without their life being in it.

* * *

Of major concern for many people as a loved one prepares to die are the issues of nutrition and hydration. Bill, the Hospice nurse, raised the issue of Dad's feeding tube on at least one occasion. Different Hospice organizations and workers have varying opinions about feeding devices and how they align with the Hospice philosophy. Many people are not aware that forcing someone to eat either naturally or artificially when they are in the dying process actually results in discomfort. When members of our family engaged in a long-distance discussion surrounding Dad's feeding tube and nutritional needs, I sent out this email.

Just like there is a birthing process there is a dying process, which Daddy is engaged in. His systems are shutting down. If he had never gone on the feeding tube and he were at this point, he would stop eating naturally because that is what people do; it is part of the dying process because their body systems are gradually shutting down.

In fact feeding people at this point in their process causes discomfort. Most likely if Dad did not have a feeding tube at this point, he would refuse most food, except a bite here or there and sips of liquid. Another consequence of feeding him is the production of waste that results in the ongoing need to change him, disrupting his rest and making him more vulnerable to skin breakdown.

At this point Dad should not be forced to try to digest a lot of food but he should be offered small quantities of both food and liquid, and he should be receiving good mouth care, keeping the gunk out of his mouth and keeping his lips moist, etc. Reducing the amount of feeding is a comfort measure for Daddy. His body just isn't functioning as it was. Feeding him at this point can also hinder him from getting on with his dying, which he - from the descriptions - seems to be working toward. Possibly as Bill suggested, he would go in the next few days but there's also a possibility this could go on for weeks.

I have had several talks with Mommy about the feeding tube and as of last week, when I left, she thought she wanted it out. However, the reality of actually removing it is much more difficult and that, as health care power of attorney, is her choice.

A solution might be to continue the feeding tube for another week and then reassess. In any case Daddy needs a peaceful environment, which it hardly sounds as if he's getting. Maybe there's a CD player on which hymns and quiet music could be played in his room."

Another issue at this juncture was Dad's capability to make decisions. He didn't seem competent at this point although earlier he certainly had been questioning if life were worth living under these conditions and, he was the one, with full understanding of its ramifications, who had requested Hospice services. Even though the Hospice nurse was predicting death in a few days, the feeding tube stayed in. Because my mother was reluctant to remove it, we all decided to support any decision she made.

* * *

Annilee surprised everyone with a visit. Carol, the sister *"on duty"* suggested that Annilee (because of her great people skills) represent all of us, and tell Dad that it would be okay to let go and say goodbye. Before this plan was carried out...there was another event.

Annilee was conversing with Juliette, the live-in aid, when Carol was upstairs, Mom, in the room next to Dad's, was entertaining friends, (two Bible translators, one she'd known from birth), both who were on leave from their work in Africa. Carol described what occurred:

Suddenly we heard a squeal. I ran downstairs and lo and behold Annilee was standing in front of Juliette, who seemed to be convulsing and screaming. I went in, to be with Mom, and Nancy and her friend went into living room to investigate. Bed-bound Mom immediately got out of bed by herself in lighting speed and took off for the living room. It was a miracle!!!! I guess Juliette had been telling Annilee a story about a lady in church who was being prayed over and was healed when the Spirit of God overcame Juliette! (Thus the squeal)

Never a dull moment here. Mom seems fine from her miracle act and Dad slept through it all. Nancy (one of the Bible translators) explained that she had seen this in Africa where it's called being slain in the spirit and now we are all pretending it never happened. Mom's first reaction was to call the agency and get someone else but we pooh poohed that. What next?

Carol went on to say that instead of taking out the feeding tube the decision had been made to cut down on the quantity of food. Dad was sleeping almost all the time and he was making it rather clear he did not like people making noise. He did, however, sporadically wake up, open his eyes and even occasionally said a word or two.

* * *

On my parents 61st wedding anniversary, July 28th, Peggy, our "adopted" older sister - who had been an integral part of our family since my parents moved into the parsonage fifty-seven years earlier - came by with supper for my mom. On every celebration, holidays, birthdays, anniversaries, Peggy, who had continued to live nearby, invariably showed up bearing food and gifts. She was eight years older than Linnea and truly another *daughter* of my dad's, and a close confidant of my mom's. She even called our father, Father Flynn. She, of course, visited with Daddy, and seeing him so weak, glassy-eyed and sleepy was very painful for her. Before she left he woke up, recognized her and graciously spoke a few words to her.

Soon after, Marilee returned along with one of her sons and her current boyfriend. So now three of the sisters were on the premises. They were able to distract my mom from all she was enduring with lively conversation. Finally, around 10:00 that night, exhausted, they all went to bed.

Five hours later the bell that had been installed for my father rang and Marilee went down to investigate. According to Carol:

When Marilee went to investigate she discovered that Juliette thought Dad was taking his last breaths and she wanted us to be with him. We all stood around groggy from sleep and she started instructing us to call out his name and touch him and talk to him. We tried but it was a bit uncomfortable. Then Annilee asked Juliette to sing and when she declined, she asked mom to pray and she gave quite a performance. This went on for about 45 minutes and then Juliette asked us to help her as she changed him. It is difficult for one person and someone needs to be handy to assist as needed.

Juliette and Marilee took leave and Mom read the Bible while Annilee and I listened. Annilee recited some verses and then we all went to bed, though it was getting light out when Annilee and I finally shut our eyes.

Marilee left around 8:00 a.m. Annilee called hospice for guidance in providing more comfort to Dad since he seems to wince and hate the changings more than usual and they sent over a very nice nurse who showed us how to put him comfortably on his side; she answered many questions. She suggested we lower the quantity of feeding and Annilee suggested we get Dr. Cox's opinion. The nurse's concern was the possibility he would retain fluids or even have it back up into his lungs, as he gets weaker and weaker; and as his digestion slows down he could be bloated and uncomfortable. Dr. Cox was called and said he would make that judgment on Wednesday when he was planning to stop in. Both Annilee and Mom feel that Dad would want his opinion and most likely follow it. Dad has his awake moments. He drifts in and out and his eyes are glassy more often than not, but, he is amazing how he can comprehend and respond appropriately mostly with 2-3 words and body language. I have found him most peaceful during awake times if there is little noise, music in background and some physical touching; he does let us know when he does not want to be touched. His hearing is acute and I try to direct Mom into other rooms or at least away from his door when she is on the phone but it's hard for her to remember this – old habits die hard. Annilee has been great with Mom who continues to be a challenge, especially trying to help her realize that she is exhausted and could use a rest. We all dozed on and off all day after the morning rush of visitors, helpers and hired help fluttered about. It must be very disconcerting for Mom when new people come and they think that she is the hospice patient. She handles it well but what must she be feeling! Oh well, time to sleep, there continues to "never be a dull moment!" We are learning to go with the flow.

* * *

Life still continued to be eventful. A night or so before the doctor was to come and assess Dad regarding his feeding tube Dad awoke around 3:00 am. He proceeded to kick off his covers and insisted on getting out of bed. He went to the table and wanted to eat. Marilee fed him some applesauce and then he had a few bites on his own. He was up for about an hour. Then he wanted to go back to bed. Both Mom and Annilee said it was difficult to judge how aware he really was because he didn't talk much. Annilee said he didn't seem to remember he had been the pastor of Nanuet Baptist Church and didn't seem to have recollection that he had been in bed for well over a week.

* * *

It is not uncommon for terminally ill patients to rally, to have a surge of energy, as death approaches. Some people who have been bed-bound for days insist on getting up; some walk around and are awake longer than they have been in days. In some cases this is termed *"terminally restlessness"* and typically occurs within several days of death.

During the afternoon after the middle of the night event, Daddy exhibited more restlessness. He was up from 2:45 – 4:15 in the afternoon but was confused. When he indicated he wanted to go back to bed, he still was restless and kept repeating, *"Don't leave, don't leave,"* so Carol sat with him while she crocheted. Later, after a nap he woke up, pulled up his blankets and stated, *"I am frozen with fear,"* but when my sister asked what he feared, he did not reply. She told him he was loved and we were caring for him and explained there were lots of people there to help him. St. Theresa arrived and apparently her presence had a calming effect and he relaxed. When Hospice was consulted, the on-call nurse recommended a quarter dropper of morphine but Mom did not like that suggestion. She claimed that morphine had sped up her sister-in-law's death.

* * *

I felt discouraged when I heard that in two instances - reducing the quantity of feeding and administering morphine - Hospice nurse recommendations were not followed. In the fifteen years I had worked as a Hospice Chaplain, I had developed incredible respect for Hospice nurses' knowledge and their ability to raise the level of comfort for patients and manage pain. From my own experience I was well aware both of these protocols were common practice at end of life.

I recognized that lots of people, including medical professionals, are reluctant to administer morphine. This is in large part due to misconceptions, like my mom's, as to how it works. In many cases before morphine is given to a patient - because the pain isn't being managed properly – the patient is suffering, and when someone is in pain it is difficult to get adequate rest. What, at times, occurs when morphine, is finally given, the patient relaxes because they are finally no longer in pain, and if they are ready, they may even relax enough to die.

Often when a person is first prescribed morphine, medical professionals are conservative in estimating the dosage because medicine affects people in various ways. It often takes professional pain management specialists several days of experimentation to arrive at the proper dosage that addresses the pain but does not overly sedate.

It always upsets me when medical professionals' placation of family members supersedes patient comfort. I believe patient comfort should be the highest priority, especially when the patients are unable to speak for themselves.

* * *

Later that night, Dad's restlessness resurfaced. He told my mother and Annilee he wanted to *"get out of here."* When they asked where he wanted to go he replied *"home."* They tried to tell him he was home. When he was asked where he thought he was, he said *"in jail."* When my sister mentioned the feeding tube his response was, *"Is that the kind of food people eat in this jail?"* When they asked him if he wanted to watch the 10:00 news he said he would when he got home.

It's very challenging communicating with someone who is near the end of their journey and going to a different realm because they are in a very different reality. At times they may be hallucinating, but they also may be in the *"thin"* place between the material and spiritual worlds.

Several weeks earlier I had sent a copy of the book, *"Final Gifts"* to the *Parsonage Medical Complex.* The book contains wonderful examples of the metaphoric language dying people often use to communicate. As a result, when I read the email about, *"the jail and going home ,"* I wrote the following:

"Did anyone get a chance to read any of the book I sent to the parsonage a couple of weeks ago called, "Final Gifts?" Dad's "talk" is classic end-of-life talk, which needs to be heard more symbolically than literally. Home could very well mean home with God. Jail could just mean being confined and not being able to get to where he wants to be, or symbolic of doing time, or whatever."

I urged them-- and in light of the exhaustion they all were experiencing, it was a big demand-- to read at least the first portion. So many family members read this book *after* the fact and wish they'd read it during their loved ones' final days. Both Annilee and Mom were able to read the initial portion of the book and it shed light on their interchanges, although no one can truly know exactly what is transpiring in the minds of those who are dying.

The doctor did pay a visit, and Dad demonstrated as much responsiveness as he had during best recent days. The doctor suggested cutting back the number of cans of feeding and recommended a quarter dropper of morphine every three or four hours for anxiety, distress or coughing.

When I heard his advice I was relieved. And since it was the doctor who made the recommendation, my mother accepted it and there was a noticeable reduction of occurrences of agitation or restlessness.

A peaceful environment is crucial for a dying person and providing one was a major challenge. Mom's bedroom was right outside Dad's; she had numerous visitors, as did he and the phone never seemed to stop ringing. This constant activity also precluded rest for the exhausted caregivers and was raising the potential for tension and unnecessary stress.

* * *

The day after the physician's visit, the feeding tube machine acted up; leaking and beeping. Theresa was called and ended up giving Dad his feedings manually. Also the caregivers began following Hospice's recommendation to precede Dad's changing times with a quarter dropper of morphine. That small step provided him with much relief and he stopped wincing during the process.

In the midst of these developments, the surgeon called Mom, out of the blue, to find out how Dad was faring. When she informed him that Dad was under Hospice and not doing well, he informed her that we needed to send Dad to the hospital or back to rehab because he was not getting the care he needed at home. He said though we were trying to care for him, Dad needed aggressive measures and he was dehydrated. Naturally my mother became very agitated and upset, not processing that the surgeon, who hadn't seen Dad in weeks, was diagnosing Dad's condition over the phone.

Once again Nurse Linnea's expertise was called for and she gave the surgeon a call, asking him what his concerns were. She explained Dad asked to go under Hospice care because he was not getting better or stronger. Additionally she thanked him for the surgery for giving him enough time to have his last book published. Though he told her he felt Dad could get better, he said since it was Dad's wishes being honored, he understood. Annilee's email response to Linnea echoed what all of us were feeling.

Linnea, Thank you for talking to Dr. C. You did a beautiful job. I loved the way you started the conversation with him. You asked him what HIS concerns were first so that he could speak his peace. Dr. C really gave his all and so I could see how this outcome would be disappointing. Still, as Linnea said, I don't think he really knew how miserable dad has been. And, Carol, if I had known the Surgeon Drama was coming, I would have stayed longer for moral support. You really had a lot on your plate the last couple of days and you have handled it wonderfully - thank you. This has been an amazing journey for all of us.

Ironically, the positive outcome of this event was that everyone truly realized that Dad was going to die no matter what, and the decisions now being made boiled down to whether to prolong the dying or let nature take its course. So after this feeding tube malfunction there was unanimous agreement not to have it re-inserted.

* * *

After not seeing my dad for three weeks, I arrived home the day after all this transpired relieved the feeding tube issue was finally resolved. Having worked for Hospice for almost 15 years, *not* feeding a person who obviously is in the dying stage, except for what they request, makes all the sense in the world to me and is unquestionably the humane thing to do. However, this is definitely a perspective that runs counter to what most people subscribe to, that food is life and we have an obligation to provide it and ingest it, or we are contributing to one's demise. Typically when I had worked with a family facing this eating issue, one of my tools of encouraging them to see things in a new way was the following story:

There was a small, young fox who one day saw a fenced vineyard with luscious fruit in it and the fox naturally wanted to go into the vineyard and eat the fruit. So it diligently put forth the effort to dig a hole, squeezed through, got into the vineyard and enjoyed the luscious fruit in the vineyard for many years. Eventually the fox sensed that it was time for him to leave the vineyard whose luscious fruit had served him well. However, over time the fox had grown considerably from eating the fruit. So the fox began eating less and less. Eventually when he was small enough he squeezed back out the hole he had dug so long ago and was able to leave the vineyard.

Thus you see the issue wasn't eating or not eating, the issue was where the fox was meant to be; the time inevitably came when it was time to leave one world and move on to another.

At that point in time no one in our family had difficulty believing that my Dad's time to leave was upon us. Now it was a matter of making it peaceful, comfortable and dignified.

* * *

Juliette, our somewhat dramatic live-in helper, was off the weekend I arrived and a soft-spoken, hard-working, tranquil woman named Veronica was substituting for her. In his semi-comatose condition, Dad seemed to receive her well.

From the time I arrived, Dad remained bed-bound and most all of the time was at peace. We gave him quarter droppers of morphine before we changed him and when we changed him, he didn't even grimace. Additionally, cutting back on his nutrition and hydration, which undoubtedly contributed to his peacefulness, meant less need for changing so we disturbed him less often. We played quiet background music and did our best to talk quietly if we were near or in his room.

My mother always had been a person who liked to plan well ahead of time whenever she could. When we were little, she'd have our Easter outfits assembled weeks before the actual holiday and when we took our annual vacation to our grandparents' houses, she'd pack our clothes so far in advance that it was a challenge finding outfits to wear in the days before we left. Because she had accepted that her husband of 61 years was dying, and because she truly did not want to see him endure any more hardship than he already had, she seemed to find relief in switching gears and she began planning Dad's funeral.

Donna and her daughter came by for a visit and she shared her reaction.

"Tara and I just got back from Nanuet. Things are very peaceful there. There is soft music playing and Dad is resting peacefully. Veronica's presence is very peaceful as well. Peggy came over for dinner and we visited on the porch after and had ice cream cake so we wouldn't bother Dad with noise.

The difference from two weeks ago is huge. Dad would open his eyes when we walked in and talked to him, but it's hard to know what's going on in his head. We would go in and just hold his hands for a while and that seemed to be very reassuring for him. Once in awhile he would say something like he wanted to go to church or what's going to happen when this is all over (Janna said he was going to be with Jesus and he said something like Jesus who?) It's hard to see him like this but at least he seems totally at peace and comfortable. And Janna is the perfect person to be with him right now. Thanks, Janna, and Linnea for being there with Mom and Dad.

* * *

My mom, now that she had something else to focus on (arrangements for my Dad even though he had not died), reverted to her Mother General mode, dispensing assignments to her troops. She had my two Ivy League educated sisters assigned to writing the obituary; she had my sister, Donna, who is good at research and project management, contact the funeral home, to find a casket for Dad; specifically the type used for Jewish burials, a basic, inexpensive wooden box. I was working on the funeral ceremony.

It was reassuring to have Linnea present, as this part of the journey with Dad was coming to a close. Her presence was a bonus in itself, but she was a much better cook than me and she got pleasure in feeding us healthfully which contributed to the wellbeing of our mother and me. It's easy during crisis situations to neglect healthy practices and the result is fewer resources to deal with an escalating situation. So, with Linnea's presence, I was not only was eating well, but also had someone to back me up so I could go running most days. However, there wasn't a whole lot that could help with the sleep deprivation.

Though it is difficult caregiving for a dying loved one, many people state, after the fact, that such experiences end up being some of the most precious of a lifetime. For me, the day-to-day routine became somewhat sacred even as it was interspersed with unsettling and precious happenings. Linnea shared one such experience with her colleagues.

"As you may know, I am home with my Father in Nanuet, in the house we grew up in. He is dying and is continuing to fade away. He is comfortable and peaceful. And I have six sisters to share this experience with.

Monday night something happened that I was so glad to be part of. He had one of his moments of near lucidity. My sister, Janna, (who is a Hospice Chaplain) and I were with him when he muttered the word "message." Janna asked him if he had a message for someone, and he nodded "No'; she asked him if he were waiting for a message from someone and he nodded "Yes." She asked whom do you need a message from and he answered "Peggy." (Peggy is like another sister to us. She lived up the street from us when we moved to Nanuet 56 years ago. She was 10 years old. I was 2 and Janna was born 3 months after we moved here.) Peggy practically grew up in our house. She became our babysitter – and still lives nearby.) Janna asked Dad if he would like to talk with

Peggy and he nodded yes. Janna called Peggy, explained what had happened and held up the phone to Dad's ear.

Dad took the phone from Janna and held it himself, and had a conversation with Peggy. He hardly has any voice, and is usually very difficult to understand. My mother asked me to get on the other line and listen. Peggy told him how much he meant to her, and asked him if he remembered that she was with him the night before. He answered, "Yes." She asked him if he knew that he was like a second father to her, and he answered, "Yes." She talked with him further, letting him know that she loved him. Then she asked him if he had had a good day or a bad day and he said, very gently and sweetly, "I had a very fine day."

All of us were extremely surprised because he had not had a conversation with anyone for the past several days in so much depth and so much lucidity and with so much clarity of voice. And this was on the phone! We talked with Peggy afterward. She was touched! Since then my dad has continued to be peaceful, but he hasn't had any more conversations and only flickers of recognition. He didn't seem to recognize Hector (Linnea's husband) *when he arrived last night.*

I am deeply sad much of the time, but it is a time for sadness. We have been planning the memorial service as a family. I feel so privileged to be a part of this special experience. Being a psychiatric nurse is very helpful in knowing that there is meaning behind words and gestures, even when they may not be clear in the moment. And the struggle to understand and respond to the meaning is well worth the effort when something like this happens.

Janna has been awesome with Dad. She helps him communicate what he wants by listening to words and phrases and looking at gestures. Last night he said he couldn't find the seminary. She assured him there would be someone there to show him the way!

* * *

This event that Linnea described, Dad needing to convey a message, turned out, though it was a number of days before he died, to be the final verbal message of his life. Interestingly he selected, not one of his own daughters but Peggy, his chosen daughter, to receive it, which actually was of great comfort to the seven of us. In some ways it was a continuation of a parental policy that my parents had always adhered to: not favoring any of us over another. Additionally, we all sensed at some level Peggy probably needed comforting words even more than any of us; so for her it was an incomprehensible gift, and just as she had so generously given so many gifts to us all our lives, this was a way to reciprocate in a momentous way.

Though spoken almost a week before he died, my father's final words, *"I've had a very fine day"* I chose to interpret as, *"I've had a very fine life."* And he did, at least until these last seven months since his surgery. I will always wonder if prior to his getting caught up in the rat race of medical intervention, would the ending had been better for him had he documented a very clear comprehensive living will that specified when that treatment be stopped because the life he was leading was no longer what he considered to be one with quality.

If he had explained that a life for him was not worth living: when eating was no longer pleasurable, when he was unable to focus enough to write, when he could not move his body from one location to another so he could comfortably nap when he wanted, and if, at that point, comfort care could have been initiated, would that have made even a finer life? Or, were there sufficient compensatory moments and events embedded in the months of anguish and frustration to redeem the suffering? Sadly we will never know the answer to those questions. But from being an observer in his experience I gleaned wisdom and will create guidelines to impact the decisions for the time I will have to face my own death.

When Susan received Linnea's description of the conversation with Peggy, she responded:

Thanks for the touching email. How wonderful that Daddy initiated contact with Peggy. Beautiful. It is reassuring to know that he is peaceful.

I am sitting in an all-day meeting with lots of men in suits listening to one presentation after another and it is very surreal to be reading your emails in this environment. I keep smashing my napkin into my eyes to try to use pressure to hold back the tears. I had to give a presentation here this morning so I am glad it is over.

* * *

The days continued with Daddy peacefully fading away. Keeping track of what day of the week was difficult with all the getting up in the night for caregiving. Sleeping also was difficult because I would wake up and wonder if Dad was still with us. Then after I ran down to check on him, and was reassured he was breathing, it was a challenge to return to sleep, even though I was bone tired. With so many people coming and going, life seemed surreal.

Here is an excerpt from my journal – *Caring for Dad is like boot camp. He has to be changed and turned and medicated every four hours. However, I am amazed how care giving can be addicting and somewhat fulfilling, along with exhausting. I am very fortunate to share this sacred time with him as he ends his life's journey."*

* * *

Though Dad was still with us, we worked on the final arrangements: Annilee and Susan wrote a very moving obituary, a beautiful and true reflection of who Dad was. Service plans, driven by Mom's wishes, continued to be created. She wanted the service to primarily consist of family members reading or speaking interspersed with musical selections.

Since the church my father served for forty years had an interim pastor who didn't know Dad, my mother, the General, decided that I should serve as the celebrant. I wasn't certain this was a good idea, to officiate at your own father's funeral, or that it was something I wanted to do. However, I'd learned by experience that usually it was less painful to obey my mom's wishes than to try to go against them, neither was the death of her soul mate the occasion to do so. Also, if I were the officiant, I could craft a service that would meet the needs of my family members whose beliefs were not as conservative as my dad's.

Although my father had accepted the ordination of women ministers, (one of his books was *"My Daughter, the Preacher"*) his church hadn't endorsed female clergy; however, no one prevented me from officiating. Undoubtedly, my mother's well-honed skills at achieving her objectives played a part. In fact, the church administrator and the music director, who had shared my dad's ministry for over thirty years, provided absolute support and assistance.

* * *

As we all are aware from personal experience, people often do not die at convenient times. Linnea and I received an email from Annilee, who was serving as spokesperson for our other sisters that started out, *"I have to say that Susan, Donna, Carol and I have been stressing about the timing of this."* She went on to explain that Carol in Sioux Falls had promised to babysit for her grandchildren the coming week, and Annilee, Donna and Susan had reservations for YMCA family camp for their family the upcoming week, a tradition that was a highlight of the year for their offspring. To sum things up, that next week was the worst possible week for all of them for a memorial service in Nanuet. Annilee asked if it would be possible, if Dad died in the next day or so, to wait and hold the service off until the following weekend.

Naturally, we reassured everyone that there was no reason to disrupt these plans to have an immediate service. The proposal was to have a private burial at the cemetery the morning before the actual service and that too could be easily postponed. Making this decision reassured everyone that they could continue with their scheduled plans.

At this point in my ministry I had officiated at more than 400 funerals, memorial services or celebrations of life and I knew from observation with numerous families how important it was to appropriately mark a death. Individuals do disservices to their surviving loved ones when they clearly mandate there be no service or celebration for them when they die, not recognizing that they are thwarting the process of grief and healing for those who have to learn to live without the presence of their loved one. Services permit survivors to acknowledge the loss, receive comfort from friends, and share feelings of sadness and grief. My sense is that not too much time should elapse between the death and the service because the gathering together is a kind of threshold for the grieving process to take root, but an extra week is not drawing things out too long.

* * *

My latest email to my sisters regarding Dad was that he continued sleeping peacefully and was, *"leaving by inches."* His hands had become mottled but were still warm to the touch. It became difficult for him to raise secretions in his throat that resulted in the sound that is commonly known as the *"death rattle."* These symptoms definitely classified his state as, *"actively dying",* which meant his death could occur anytime, from hours to days. Truly, Dad was just fading away.

After I had been covering at the parsonage for a week, the following email came from Carol. *"Janna, Linnea, and Mom, I bet this has been the longest week of your lives! Even though I am not there and I am trying to keep my mind occupied with the business of the days, it has been a long week for me. I think of you all often and know that this time with dad and mom, going through this process will have lasting effects on you and you will be able to*

relate to people in ways others cannot imagine...Do take
care of each other and yourselves. Hugs to you!"

There were a flurry of emails from the sisters who were
heading to Family Camp, communicating ways they could
be contacted because the camp was located in a remote
area five or six hours away and it had questionable cell
coverage. The families prepared for their much anticipated
annual fun time together with mixed feelings, knowing this
family camp gathering the memory of the sweet time would
be tainted with a sorrowfulness because of dad's dying.

As it turned out we did not need all the emergency
number preparation. I had parked myself in my Dad's sick
room after dinner and had been there several hours.
Everyone else had gone to bed when... Dad peacefully
stopped breathing. Whatever it was that had animated
him with earthly life had departed noiselessly without
fanfare. After I spent a few moments prayerfully in the
sacred space of my father's passing, I awoke my mother
and got Linnea and informed them Dad had stopped
breathing.

Though we all were aware this would happen, and
though I had experience being in the presence of someone
breathing his or her last breath, it was still jarring, neither
did it seem real. This was not one of my residents or
patients, this was my one and only father.

We called Hospice and notified all the sisters. Because,
by this time it was rather late, we decided to make the call

to the funeral home, but hold off until morning to notify other relatives and close friends.

It took almost an hour for the funeral personnel to come. A man and woman arrived impressively dressed in professional attire. They were a married couple and had worked many funerals at the local funeral home with my Dad. We discovered they had been at a party and when they learned that Pastor Flynn had died, instead of coming as they were, they went home and dressed in a very dignified way, because they wanted to demonstrate a worthy tribute to a man whose dignity and integrity they admired.

Bearing witness to professional pallbearers conveying the body of a loved one away from the place he called home for the very last time is beyond heartrending. Already exhausted emotionally and physically, I dropped into bed barely finding the energy to change out of my clothes.

Celebrating a Life Well-Lived

Since the interment and memorial service were not scheduled for a full week, Linnea and her husband decided to return to Chicago. The live-in caregiver also returned home leaving just my mother and me at the parsonage. I think, for both of us, the increased potential for peace and quiet was therapeutic. Of course, there were numerous calls and visitors, decisions to make, arrangements to finalize, and plenty to keep us focused on everyday affairs. I remember thinking that having this week's respite probably was beneficial because rather than having eight decision makers trying to come to consensus, my mother and I could more easily attend to the business at hand. We already had recruited members of the family to participate in the memorial service, so with the help of the church administrator and music minister we crafted a celebration we hoped did justice to my father's remarkable life.

* * *

My intense feelings about the importance of a first-class goodbye undoubtedly stem from the experiences of my own life. I was fourteen, a vulnerable age, when my seventh sister, Tricia, was born. She lived less than a day and our family never celebrated her life, or acknowledged her death. As a "favor" to my Dad, a local undertaker buried her in an unmarked grave in a local cemetery.

A decade and a half later, when Christopher, my two month old son died, we didn't celebrate his life either, and - as happened in the past - a funeral director in my husband's hometown did us a "favor" and buried Christopher, unmarked, in the local cemetery.

These deaths occurred in the 1960's and 1970's before our society, including funeral professionals, clergy and psychologists, had learned the toll unresolved grieving could exact on families. However, retrospectively I realize that I detected - even when I was only fourteen, and then again in my mid-twenties – that failing to acknowledge the loss of life was psychologically and spiritually unhealthy. You cannot heal what you do not acknowledge.

Though we did nothing publicly to honor Christopher's life, in the days after the numbness wore off, I did a lot of journaling, writing and cross country skiing. Instinctively I must have sensed that these pastimes were therapeutic in acknowledging and moving through my pain.

* * *

My father had always believed funeral and memorial services should be brief so we decided to limit the service to an hour, although twenty minutes probably would have been more to his liking. Basically, besides me doing a eulogy, my mother chose to limit the speakers to two other people: one was a pastor who had been the son my father never had, a man my dad had mentored and who currently served as senior minister of a megachurch out of state, and the other was Susan, my youngest sister.

To acknowledge my father's Irish heritage, the music director was able to recruit an Irish tenor to sing. Thus the service opened with a moving rendition of *"Danny Boy."* An unexpected gift that really enhanced the service was the musical performance of a young man who had been a member of the church, and who had gone on to be a world famous violinist. When he heard of my father's death, he contacted the minister of music and offered to perform. And we decided that *The Hallelujah Chorus*, led by the church choir, was our choice as an appropriate upbeat finale. My father had lived an exceptionally fine, long life and deserved a first-class and upbeat finale. Well over three hundred people came to the service.

One comment I received which I am still unclear as to the meaning was, *"Had I known the funeral was going to be like this, I would have brought my kids!"* In any case, it felt like we had done a fitting job of celebrating the life of this very special man. During the occasion we had the opportunity to be reunited with friends and family from far and near, and once the service ended, we all felt like a milestone in this long journey had been attained.

Meaning, it's common, after the conclusion of a

meaningful memorial celebration, that family members and loved ones feel an emotional shift. It's not accurate to label what happens *"closure"* because in actuality there is never closure when it comes to acclimating to a death. Each milestone achieved in the grieving process is like arriving at the end of a movement in a classical music symphony in which there is a pause before another segment begins. It doesn't necessarily translate to feeling better, but it often feels as if something internally has shifted.

* * *

The morning of the funeral, about forty or so of us - family and those considered family - had gathered to bury Dad in the cemetery located a block from the parsonage, and a block from the church. I would have loved - as an assembly - to walk behind a hearse bearing my father to the burial site because there is something very rudimentary and therapeutic in physically accompanying a loved one to their final resting place. My mother, however, preferred to keep the burial part of the remembrance private.

A few years earlier, my parents had purchased two cemetery plots in this town they had called home for 60 years. At the time my dad had quipped, *"I finally made my first real estate investment."* So that summer morning, gathered around his casket, on the first piece of land Dad had ever owned, we shared memories, listened to music and adorned his coffin with red roses.

In the front of the group of those who loved him most was his eldest granddaughter, great with child. Realizing that most probably her son would receive the breath of life around the same time that his great-grandfather would have turned eighty-eight years old, provided some consolation in a painful time. Life, as they say, is cyclical.

Often as we journey with loved ones during their dying time, memories surface that have long been long forgotten. Sitting on the front porch of the house where my Dad lived his last fifty-seven years, I remembered that in my childhood a towering elm tree used to grace the end of the sidewalk. It was strong, beautiful, and provided sanctuary from the hot sun. One of my father's rituals was, at lunchtime, to carry his youngest daughter to the tree, to touch its leaves and feel its breeze before putting her down for her nap.

That tree no longer exists; no physical evidence of its presence remains. Yet, the gifts it gave in its lifetime will forever endure. During its time of existence it served and lived its purpose.

Though my father was no longer physically with us, his spirit would live on as we allow him to be remembered in our lives; which means the fruitfulness of the life he lived will endure. When our loved ones die, we can be thankful not only for what they meant while in our lives, but also for what they continue to be after they've crossed over.

Life, to me, is not only cyclical, it is also continuous. Often in an ending that seems so absolute, therein lies a new beginning. The anguish of one closing can be the precursor to a new opening in our lives.

* * *

Each person processes grief in his or her own ways. Here is part of what Annilee shared after she returned home after the funeral. *"I have been completely wallowing in emotion yesterday and today. Yesterday I watched the DVD of pictures created by the funeral home several times and just cried and cried. When Dad finally died, I experienced relief more than sadness. But as I watched the DVD to the music of his favorite hymn, "How Great Thou Art," I just sobbed and sobbed. Watching him grow up and get married and proudly hold his first baby and then see all his little girls grow up and then see him become a grandfather just made me cry with thankfulness for the ways he had experienced many of the blessings of life – a sense of joy that he would call, "common grace of God" and experience in such full measure. But there's also a sense of sadness that it is over. I felt so glad that our parents stayed together from the time they were in their bloom on their honeymoon until Dad was playing ball with their twenty-second grandchild. I felt so happy that our family had gathered together through all the years – that the seven sisters could be together with mom and dad*

— first as little girls and then as young women and then as middle-aged women.

And then it hit me that Dad would never be in a family photo again. I felt so full of sadness – a literal feeling of, "What is wrong with this picture?" It is like there is a gaping hole. He was the only guy we had and I miss him. So it is weird how I can be so relieved that he was released from the body that was no longer serving him and also feel so sad that his life is over and that he won't be in our family anymore."

In an email I wrote after returning to my life in Virginia I said, *"People here are being so nice to me that it's almost making it more painful."* One of my residents at the retirement community asked where they could send donations. I designated the Hospice House where I served as chaplain and word must have spread because over $1500 was donated in memory of my Dad. It was incredibly touching and great balm to my sorrow.

* * *

Several of my sisters were able to remain for a week or so with my mom, attending to paperwork and putting a plan in place for her safety. She installed a "Lifeline" alert button, basically to appease her daughters, and chose a gravestone for Dad that she would eventually share. Along with his name and birth and death dates, she also had her name and birthdate inscribed. Apparently though, as is very common for people who are grieving to not think clearly, she authorized her birthdate to be October 28 rather than what it was, October 31st. She never enjoyed sharing her birthday with trick-or-treaters so we always wondered if this was her way of procuring herself a new birthday, one other than Halloween.

In circumstances of slow and trying passings, typically there is some relief when the end actually comes, and a total reorientation of perception from uncertainty and waiting, to a measure of being able to change course and move on. It's like being stranded on a ship anchored in the deep with no timetable and then all of a sudden the anchor is released, and you have a say again in where you are headed.

My mother possessed a lot of inner strength and fortunately physically she was also stronger than she had been, but she needed additional props in place being wheelchair bound and living alone. After the previous eight months of chaos and uncertainty my mother seemed ready for a less stressful life. She hired St. Theresa, who had become more like a family member than a helper, to chauffer her around when she wanted and needed to get out of the house. My sisters and I initiated the plan for each of us to take a day of the week to call home and check in. Because my mom was sharp mentally, her safety awareness was excellent, and she wasn't fearful of being alone in the house, we all felt comfortable with her situation.

* * *

Walking the forested trail in the park across from our Williamsburg, Virginia townhouse had become part of my weekend routine in the months after I returned home from my father's funeral. The county cleared the area and opened the hiking path in 2006, during the fall following my father's death. The first time I discovered the trail most of the leaves had dropped off the trees and the landscape was dismal, resonating with my grieving spirit. I walked the leaf-strewn path on weekends that fall, and continued walking it through the dead and cold of winter while pondering the hollowness of my spirit in the aftermath of losing a parent. I continued to walk the path, noticing the first buds of spring, promising an array of color and beauty. I kept on walking in the heat of the summer into another fall, and bit-by-bit I came to understand that it's not necessarily time that heals the pain of loss, but in time the way a bereaved person feels, can change. The initial despair and desolate barrenness gradually evolve into hope and a desire to engage more fully in life.

I hoped and prayed that all of our family members, but especially my mother, were finding their own grieving implements and paths capable of moving them from our shared experience of pain and loss to rejuvenated ways of encountering and engaging the life that is present and the one that is yet to come. Each one of us, though forever changed by this experience of loss, would need to find their own way through the journey of grief in order to eventually be fused with resources that were life nourishing because it is in tending to our own grieving hearts that we discover healing and blessing.

Janna Flynn Roche

PART II

My Mother's Story

Janna Flynn Roche

Living Alone

The life my parents shared began on the 28th of July 1945 the day a B-29 bomber smashed into the Empire State Building in New York City. Sixty years later these are some words my father penned to my mom, just months before he began his dying journey..

"It has been a wonderful life!! An unbelievable 60 years. I want to stay at 32 Highview (the address of their home) *with you, for to be with you at 32 is to be in heaven on earth. Knowing your penchant and preferences for short sermons, I end here, assuring you that I would do it all over again. I LOVE YOU !!!"*

* * *

Our mother, the Mother General, thrived on organization and the delegation of her home management system bore semblance to Frank B. Gilbreth's administrative style described in *Cheaper By the Dozen*. She required each of her daughters to perform a tremendous amount of work around the house. Every Saturday each of us was assigned a list of chores that typically took two to three hours, depending on our age. We also set the dinner table and took turns cleaning up. I certainly was aware that my sisters and I carried a much heavier load on the household duties front than any of our friends. In fact, once I reached a certain age, I don't remember actually seeing my mother do housework, other than laundry and cooking, until her nest emptied. She was the overseer and we were the worker bees.

My parents were very careful in their attempts to treat us all equally. For example, when my older sister - who was married in the late sixties - got one thousand dollars to pay for her wedding, that set the standard for the amount designated for the rest of us. A thousand dollars for wedding expenses, even in the sixties, meant a lot of creative engineering but fifteen years later, when the youngest sister tied the proverbial knot, with a member of a prominent Washington, D.C. family, a thousand dollars was a joke. Inflation aside, fairness meant we all were issued the same amount.

Though treating us equally in some ways, my parents simultaneously encouraged individualism; recognizing that each of us was unique in forging our own pathways in life. In fact, my mother used to verbalize what she felt were the admirable traits each of us possessed. Consequently she encouraged us to pursue our skills and talents. One of us she deemed "clever;" I was the organized one, and so on. The encouragement we received was appreciated, but there were times when it was difficult to distinguish between fulfilling her wishes or our own. Also, if my mother dubbed someone with a specific quality, like organized or clever, that kind of meant the descriptor was taken and no longer available for anyone else

* * *

Prior to my dad's illness, he had been my mother's caregiver. She had been largely wheelchair bound since her mid-seventies, but that didn't prevent my parents from spending weeks or a couple of months each winter in Hawaii. She walked some, but only would do so if a person actually physically supported her. She eschewed walkers, deeming them inept because they would not prevent her from falling backwards. She suffered from osteoporosis and was eventually diagnosed with ataxia; a lack of balance. Utilizing a wheelchair was a proactive safety measure she initiated to prevent possible falls. She could transfer herself into cars, beds, onto the toilet, and into her wheelchair. Her legs were strong enough to navigate the wheelchair around rooms, but she was unable to climb a flight of stairs so couldn't access the upper levels of the parsonage.

Prior to constraining herself to the wheelchair she had endured some serious injuries. On two different occasions she shattered a shoulder, resulting in surgical replacements, one a full replacement and the other a partial. She'd also suffered numerous compression fractures in her back. Though she'd always been a healthy eater and a milk-drinker, these injuries were sustained in the days prior to physicians proactively recommending calcium supplements, particularly for small-boned women who have experienced eight full-term pregnancies.

During her recovery periods from these incidents when she was unable to navigate the two steps to the downstairs toilet, my dad served as her caregiver, which he claimed was his retirement vocation. He carried out his duties with his usual good humor. I can remember the occasion when I called home one day and he said, *"Just a minute. I have to empty your mother's commode."* And then he added, *"Jesus had it easy; all he had to do was wash feet."*

Except for relatively minor concerns and the additional compression fractures suffered during my father's final days, my mother's health, for someone in her 80's, had been stable for several years and as she began her life as a widow this continued to be the case. Periodically, there were issues to be addressed that necessitated one of the daughters be in residence for a few days. We continued to make our phone calls on our assigned days and all of us tried to visit as frequently as our schedules permitted so there wouldn't be extended periods without a daughter's support. But overall, in her recently widowed period, my mother - with the assistance of friends, volunteers and paid help - fared well, living alone.

* * *

After my husband and I made several moves, when my son was in grammar school, my son had said, *"You know, Mom, whenever we move, some things get better and some things get worse."* My young philosopher had put his finger on a very important truth. In any life change, whether desired or not, whether chosen or not, some things improve and some worsen.

From counseling newly bereaved widow(er)s, I had learned that this is even true after the loss of a beloved long-time life partner. For most widowed people, clearly, the negative changes dominate, but for those able to admit it, there are some things that get better. At times the improvement is in the freedom to make choices about how time and money are spent, but often the positive change means not having to factor in another person's wants in the daily activities of life – what and when to eat, when to go to bed, etc. sometimes, for the first time in their adult lives.

For a significant number of people who have lost their spouses, particularly those in the cohort of the Greatest Generation, widowhood is the first experience they have ever had of living alone. This was true for my mom. During her college years she'd lived at home, and then married my father a month after she graduated, so sixty plus years later she found herself, in her early 80's, living alone for the very first time.

Though being on her own was a deficit, (I can only imagine how difficult this loss was for her) it also gave her the chance to transform loneliness into solitude; providing the opportunity to discover the benefits of living life to her own rhythm and harvesting a rich inner world. My mother had always been able to bloom where she was planted and over time she was able to discover contentment in this new lifestyle, a way of life that was very different from her previous one. It proved to be a kind of elder life sabbatical.

One of the activities my six sisters and I sacrificed during those years of caregiving was our sisters-only weekends. In the 1990's, when our ages ranged from the late thirties to early fifties - middlescence - when we all were peaking in our personal and professional obligation eras, the seven of us began the tradition of gathering annually for a long weekend. Early on, those sisters' weekends were held in Chicago, at Linnea's twenty-eighth story condo, overlooking Lake Michigan. Not only was Chicago a central location, and an easy hub to access, but also Linnea had sufficient sleeping accommodations in her couch-laden living room to accommodate all of us.

Moreover, the Windy City is a venue of fun excursions and activities and it was in close proximity to where my mother was raised, where cousins still resided. These gatherings were highly anticipated and oases in our lives, occasions for us to just be ourselves, to laugh and do things together as grown-ups without spouses and children. Undoubtedly, these weekends, though short in duration, reinforced our sister bond.

However, once our parents began to have health concerns, that necessitated us increasing our visits to their New York home, we suspended sister gatherings. The suspension stayed in effect after my Dad died because any discretionary time anyone of us had, needed to be dedicated to upholding mom in New York so she could continue to successfully live alone in her own house.

My mother made it clear that she wanted to remain in the parsonage so she acclimated to her new life alone; transferring herself from bed, to wheelchair, to toilet and pulling herself to a standing position when necessary to prepare food or bathe herself. St. Theresa chauffeured her to medical appointments and occasionally the two went out to lunch. Mom organized what, for her, was a life with quality, staying connected with friends far and wide by phone and mail. She communicated with family via email but also maintained a significant amount of U.S. mail correspondence with long-time friends. During these years, she wrote a book of memoirs, *Serendipitously I Roll*, that she self-published.

Writing was not a new past time for my mother. Over the years, she had numerous articles published in religious publications and also co-authored two books with my dad.

One of the family traditions she initiated, when we were all still living at home, was sending out an annual Christmas letter each holiday season. I'd been maintaining Mother General's Christmas letter mailing list for a number of years, but actually writing, printing and mailing these letters had become a major and somewhat expensive ordeal that involved several of her daughters because there were over five hundred names on her list. Over the span of her life, she had been faithfully maintaining these connections and doing so continued to give her a great deal of pleasure.

Mom's eighty-fifth birthday fell the year after Dad's death. As a surprise to her, my sisters and I sent out a letter to her five hundred plus mailing list friends and family, informing them of this birthday milestone and inviting them to call or send a card sometime during her birthday month.

I happened to be home early in October that year when the bombardment of visits, phone calls, deliveries and letters began. People my mother hadn't heard directly from in years called or visited. Gifts arrived daily at the door and in the mail. And, she received hundreds of pieces of mail. Not only was witnessing this display of affection heart-warming, it also reaffirmed that she certainly was not without a support network.

Mom's closest and most valued friend was Peggy, our adopted older sister. When their relationship began - my mom was in her twenties and Peggy was ten - it had been one of a mentor and mentee, but this was no longer the case. In these later years after a lifetime of connection, Peggy and Mom were each other's closest confidants and

Peggy was probably the closest thing my mom had to a sister. Peggy was generous, giving and supportive, but sadly in her late sixties, she began experiencing some debilitation as a result of having contracted polio in her childhood.

My husband and I were shocked when we went home for Thanksgiving, the second year after my Dad's death, and met Peggy for dinner. When she walked into the restaurant she was bent over and walked with her face almost parallel to the ground, making us wonder how she was able to drive a car. Not one to complain, Peggy determinedly did not allow her infirmity to keep her from maintaining her lifestyle as best she could, selflessly spending the majority of her days doing acts of faithful service for others and maintaining her cherished family farmhouse, the place she had lived her entire life.

Peggy had been present with my mom and me during much of the week following my father's death. She was there when the local funeral director came by to meet with my mom and have some forms signed. Peggy and the undertaker were acquainted because, upon their deaths, she had entrusted the care of her dad, her mom, and most recently her husband, to his funeral home. I don't remember much of the interchange Peggy and the Funeral Director had that afternoon, but I do recall Peggy glibly proclaiming that she had no intention of departing from her house for good, until he came to pick up her dead body.

The day after our dinner together, Peggy experienced shortness of breath and she was taken to the local hospital in an ambulance. She spent a number of days in the hospital until she improved enough to be moved to a rehabilitation center. During the time she was rehabilitating, her mental status became altered. My sisters and I had bizarre phone conversations with her during which she didn't make a whole lot of sense. It didn't seem as if anyone knew what was really going on but eventually, much to her relief, she was released and returned to her home with twenty-four hour care, a situation she considered an improvement over the rehab center, although having someone stationed in her house all the time too was trying for her.

It was a major shock to all members of our family, along with Peggy's circle of friends, that soon after her arrival home, she died in her sleep. Poignantly her death occurred a little after Christmas, a holiday she had always celebrated with passion.

All of us were devastated that our beloved Peggy was gone, but my mother particularly and understandably found this loss to be unbearable. Peggy was not only someone my mother could be herself with, she also was accessible, available, supportive and a liaison with the church trustees in parsonage maintenance issues. In addition, she clearly had been the single most important presence in my mom's everyday life after the death of our father. I don't think the idea of a world without Peggy in it, was something my mother, or any of us, ever imagined. Our adopted sister had always been a significant part of our family's life, and her death, at only sixty-eight years old, and in such close time proximity to my father's death, was devastating.

All of my sisters and I came home for Peggy's Memorial Service. And all of us were heartbroken, as was my mother. However, the way my mother handled her emotional pain was by striking out and making life difficult for those closest to her. By this time, two of my sisters had been training to become Massage Therapists, so my memory of the few days surrounding Peggy's service was the ongoing sequence of taking turns - two at a time - downstairs enduring my mother's tirades, and then rotating upstairs to receive a reward massage from one of our sisters before we had to return for our next go round. Eventually, of course, my mother calmed down, and was able to reconcile herself to this traumatic loss. It appears she was able - in time - to do a lot of her grieving by talking with her friends on the telephone about Peggy, which empowered her to make sense of all that had transpired. But clearly Peggy's death left my mother with an indelibly wounded heart.

In retrospect it appeared that my mother coped much better with the loss of my father than with the loss of Peggy, surely, at the time, the two most important people in her life. The difference in her response perhaps was due, in large part, to the suddenness of Peggy's death. My mother had no time to anticipate this traumatic event and probably never considered out-living her beloved Peggy.

Grief, experts will tell us, is something that everyone does in his or her own way and no one knows ahead of time how they will react to a loss. However, when a death is sudden and unexpected it often creates a more difficult grieving process in comparison to a loss someone has time to anticipate. And, when someone suffers multiple deaths of significant people in a short expanse of time, that too exacerbates the grief work that is required for reconciliation to the losses.

* * *

For close to five years after Dad's death, Mom's health remained relatively stable but in her late eighties she began experiencing some serious heart issues. A pacemaker was implanted to prompt her heart to beat, which helped, but then she received a diagnosis of aortic stenosis, a condition only treatable with open-heart surgery; a procedure my mother was too frail to endure even if she had been willing. After an event, when she passed out and was rushed to the local Emergency Department, and given some tests, a cardiologist tersely informed her that she had a twenty-five percent chance of still being alive in two years. She definitely was becoming more fragile and as a result of the earlier shoulder surgeries, arthritis set in which impacted her ability to transfer herself from bed to toilet, etc. Following a hospitalization, she was discharged to rehab, ending up in the same nursing facility where my father had spent four months, a place that did not evoke fond memories for her, nor contribute to a swift recovery. This institutionalization weakened her in body and spirit and eventually, when she could return home - and being able to do so at times seemed dubious - her medical situation was considerably more precarious.

Calling in Hospice

During this time of ill health my mother periodically lost interest in eating and for her that brought back memories of managing my father's ingestion issues. Finding herself in a situation where eating was repulsive, she lamented that she had not been as sympathetic to the distress my dad was experiencing when she admonished him for not eating enough.

In time she grew more frail, required oxygen to breathe, and her physician recommended she go under Hospice Care. As it appeared to be, she took this as a death sentence and though eventually she came to truly enjoy and appreciate the Hospice staff that served her, initially acknowledging that her condition was terminal, was understandably difficult for her. In many ways she had admirable inner strength and an upbeat take on life, but when she experienced severe emotional pain, she initially displayed hurtful behavior to others, particularly those in her own family.

Which meant during this time period, as she was acclimating to the idea of dying, it was extra trying for all of us. To make matters worse, soon after engaging their services, the Hospice team said that if she wanted to remain in her own home, she would require twenty-four hour care. This, justifiably, was another devastating blow to my fiercely independent mother.

* * *

I visited the most highly recommended long-term care facility near Mom's home when it was determined that she could no longer live on her own. My visit triggered the realization that the suburban area she lived in didn't have desirable facilities for long-term care, particularly for someone who is mentally competent and gregarious. In my capacity as a healthcare chaplain, I had attended meetings, over the years, in various long-term facilities around the state of Virginia and it became clear to me that Virginia had more desirable options. There was an outstanding CCRC (continuing care retirement community) in Richmond, I'd been to a number of times, that I felt would give my mom good quality-of-life. After researching it, I discovered that depending on availability, the facility occasionally accepted direct-admission residents to their convalescent center, even when the individual hadn't bought into independent living options. Though the cost was comparable to the less desirable options in New York, this facility was very expensive. However, because my mother had lived frugally on my father's Social Security at the parsonage since his death, she had sufficient resources to qualify financially.

My sisters, Annilee and Susan, who lived about an hour and a half north of Richmond, met me one day at the facility for an appointment and tour with the marketing manager. Both sisters were suitably impressed. Not only, if my mother were admitted, would she have a private room in convalescent - because all their rooms were private - she also would be allowed access to all the activities of Independent Living, and the selection of opportunities was impressive.

The facility housed a large auditorium where dancing companies, musical groups and other professional entertainers were booked for performances. It had several resident-run thrift stores offering clothing, household items, and furniture, where Mom could do some shopping - a past time she'd always enjoyed - especially when it involved a bargain. And, because the facility was faith-based, there were daily religious services on site. The facility also had an array of clubs, physical fitness classes and other opportunities. But, more importantly, their dining policy was flexible. Residents - even those residing in the convalescent center - were not assigned specific dining venues; provided they could eat without assistance. In other words, as long as she could get herself to where she desired to be, my mother would have access to all the resources the community offered residents, no matter which level of care. This flexibility opened up possibilities for many interesting friendships.

This lifestyle, for a nursing or convalescent center resident, is uncommon. Most care centers with various levels of care, from independent to nursing, restrict residents either intentionally or because their facilities are not laid out to be free flowing. Very few encourage residents to mingle outside their own level of care.

Before my sisters and I made our visit, my mother, who had by then become a great proponent and user of Google, began researching this community and after looking into other retirement communities (where various friends lived), she realized what the Richmond community offered was exceptional.

Following our on-site visit, Annilee and Susan shared aspects of the incredible quality of life the CCRC offered. After much soul-searching, my mother decided moving to Virginia was preferable to having a caregiver in her home twenty-four hours a day. Plus, the close proximity of three of her daughters to this new home was an added bonus. It had been years since any of us lived that close to our parents' residence.

The admission procedure was intense, and my sisters and I joked about how the system was similar to applying to an Ivy League College. Mom had to have an interview, which was conducted over the phone. The fact that she was under Hospice Care caused us to worry she would be disqualified but it turned out to be a non-issue.

In early January, word was received that Mom had been accepted for admission. That meant she only had a few weeks to make the move and take up residence.

Living in Virginia

I couldn't imagine what the whole experience must have been like for my mother. Here she was, eighty-nine years old, and, in a sense, being forced to leave the home she'd lived in for over 60 of those years. On top of that, she was moving to a brand-new state, community and culture where she knew no one, and she was doing it as a Hospice patient, meaning she was expected to die within six months. She had always been extremely practical and part of the basis for her decision rested on the fact that her support network in New York was failing. The number of friends who were still alive was dwindling and the few who remained were too frail to be of assistance; many individuals she'd counted on previously were relocating themselves. So she recognized there was little left for her, if she chose to stay where she was.

* * *

Fortunately, Mom's resilient spirit and inner strength surfaced and she seemingly made the decision to treat this relocation as an adventure. When I was sharing a meal with her in the dining room, not long after she became a resident, the Executive Director of the CCRC stopped by our table and informed me that it took my mother about one hour to acclimate to her new home. Her adjustment was remarkable and before long she was popular not only among the staff but also with other residents.

Of course, life in Virginia was not without challenges, but my mother came to love her new surroundings and cultivated many new friendships. She enrolled in a pottery class, a craft she'd never previously attempted, and she attended every event on the calendar that she could. After six years of quiet solitude, apparently she was ready to open herself to a more stimulating existence.

Interestingly, several months after her move, my mother's health improved and it was deemed she no longer was hospice-appropriate. In other words, her heart disease wasn't progressing and the medical profession could no longer justify a prognosis that she would die within six months. Thus, she was discharged from Hospice care, which was bittersweet for her because it meant the discontinuation of visits from nurses, social workers, a chaplain and a wonderful volunteer, (who actually never stopped visiting), but it also signified she could expect to live longer with the life of quality she was enjoying.

For the next year and a half Mom's heart problems did not resurface and she had no hospitalizations. As she told her friends she found life so enjoyable that it almost was as if she were on a continuous cruise.

* * *

The following is a copy of the annual holiday letter sent to her five hundred mailing list friends her second Christmas in Virginia.

"My ninth great-grandchild was born this past year. Other than that, my life has been uneventful and that very uneventfulness is newsworthy. At 91, the fact that I enjoyed a year of good health is not to be taken for granted.

"Live life well," is the motto of Westminster Canterbury. I have lived well this year. My worldly possessions are whittled down to fit into one room. While paring down my possessions was difficult at first, I now feel that the simplicity of having only a roomful of things to keep track of is liberating. I have the run of a beautiful building with libraries, parlors, and dining rooms that are someone else's job to maintain.

My daily life is full of activities that nourish me physically, mentally, socially, and spiritually. Benedictine monks believe that a balanced life should include five practices: labor, study, hospitality, renewal, and prayer. Upon reflection, I realize that my daily life includes all five practices.

At my age, propelling myself from place to place in my wheelchair and keeping on top of the logistics of life require enough physical and mental energy to count as "labor." While I don't have a formal course of "study," I read voraciously and am always learning new things in my Bible study group, book club, and the lectures offered here. Visits with family and friends offer ample opportunities for "hospitality." I experience "renewal" through making pottery, going to musical concerts, and trips to the thrift shop in the basement. Finally, my day includes private "prayer" and I regularly attend Evensong and healing services in the chapel. This chapter of my life feels more simple, balanced, and prayerful than the busier, more frenetic chapters of my youth. And yes, there are challenges in this chapter of life. Living in a long-term care facility means that I am up close and personal with death and diminishment. Sadly, on several occasions this year, I learned of the unexpected death of another resident with whom I had been chatting only hours before he or she died. These experiences have reminded me that every human encounter is precious, and now I try to be more present in my routine interactions with everyone.

In the dining room, I often see a man tenderly spoon-feed his mother. It takes an hour and a half for her to complete the meal. I feel blessed to see what genuine love looks like in a very intense and specific way. Every day I see many examples of this type of love in action here.

I realize that our diminishments provide opportunities for qualities such as steadfastness, kindness, patience, and fidelity to come forth. Our physical reality by its very nature is full of heartbreaking limitations, but it is the hard edges of these limitations that allow us to experience the unlimited divine love and peace available to us.

May you experience God's unlimited love, joy, and peace in 2014.

* * *

The City of Richmond was a much more central and convenient location for all the sisters (except the one living in New York) to make more frequent visits. We discovered going to see our mother was more relaxing because meals were prepared by the staff and visits could be spent exploring her wonderful community that opened more possibilities for engaging activities than the parsonage in New York offered.

Our mother had always envied our sister weekends so for the two years she resided at her retirement community; we resumed our sisters' weekends, making her CCRC our destination so she could be included. Her facility had excellent guest accommodations, good food and a multitude of places where we could gather and view pictures and family videos. Our mother enjoyed showcasing her seven daughters and we enjoyed meeting her friends, shopping in the thrift store and being together in a nourishing environment.

A fear my mother had was that once she was no longer under Hospice Care she would have to visit doctors frequently. She, at this stage in life, had little faith that their medication and aggressive treatment would do her any good. She was a minimalist when it came to prescription medication and believed doctors' interventions were often more harmful than helpful. Fortunately with the assistance of the facility medical director and the twenty-four hour nursing staff, off campus medical appointments were kept to a minimum.

Mom was very content not leaving the CCRC. Riding in the wheelchair van was bumpy and painful and she found the process of being put on and taken off the transport van anxiety producing. Additionally, she didn't have a lot of faith in physicians, particularly when it came to caring for the elderly.

So life was about the best it could be for her and my mother embraced it as fully as possible. Having arrived in a brand new environment at age eighty-nine knowing no one, she made the most of her surroundings. She experimented with new activities, found ways to nourish herself, and formed special bonds with a variety of individuals. Unlike many people at her stage in life, especially those who find themselves in somewhat frail conditions, she didn't choose to withdraw but embraced what life had to offer with enthusiasm and zest and discovered renewed fulfillment and meaning.

For my part, though I was now geographically the closest daughter, which translated to the on-call daughter, I found these years much more relaxing as a caregiver than when she'd been in her own home in New York. Though my visits were more numerous, they didn't involve having to request time off from work and could be made during weekends and evenings. More importantly my mother was in an environment where my sisters and I believed her caregivers were trustworthy and her welfare was truly being addressed with dignity and compassion.

Contrasting this with my father's experience in New York, this contentment and relief on all of our parts was not taken for granted.

Most of my sisters even stopped making the weekly calls on the assigned days because more likely than not, my mother was out and about, and not in her room near her phone. The calls we did make often ended up as voice mail messages. Contrastingly, when she'd lived alone in her house, a good portion of her day had been spent talking to friends and family on the telephone. Friends she'd conversed with in the past had less contact with her, although she still maintained an impressive amount of correspondence. It was common to have the staff members who delivered her mail ask if it was a special occasion because they often commented they'd never seen a resident get the volume of mail my mother did.

When I was visiting my mother one afternoon, about two years into her residency, a long-time neighbor and friend - who was a few years older than my mom - called. She had relocated to a facility in Massachusetts, near her son. As they were chatting all of a sudden my mother spouts out, *"Harriet, are you going to be cremated?"* It was somewhat disarming and humorous to me but I had no idea how Harriet would react. Apparently she just moved right into the topic and responded to my mother.

When the call ended, my mother brought up the subject of cremation with me. Obviously, she had been pondering this topic and stated that though she planned to be buried with Dad in the cemetery plot in New York, she felt it was a waste of money to have her body transported in a coffin from Virginia. So she'd been contemplating the idea of being cremated so there would be no cost involved in transporting her remains, because I could provide that service. She asked me to research cremation in the Richmond area, and also to poll my sisters regarding their feelings on the subject.

I did both and after further discussion with my mother, pre-arrangements for cremation were made and documented with the facility. All of my sisters were on board with my mother making any decisions she wanted regarding her burial arrangements. We were just glad she was willing to let us know her wishes.

Having dealt with numerous bereaved children as they worked on arrangements after their parents' deaths, I have come to believe that in most cases it is a great gift for survivors to have some prior instruction from the recently deceased. If the person cares about how things are handled and has specific wishes, they should be shared and documented with family members and/or the executor of the estate. Or, if a person doesn't have specific desires that also should be documented so the surviving loved ones do not agonize over whether or not they are following their final wishes. It is particularly unhelpful for someone to mandate that there be no celebration-of-life service or event, because most people need to mourn the loss of those important in their lives. And when all is said, funerals and services are truly for the living, not for the person who has died.

* * *

One activity we engaged in when visiting Mom was helping her with her wardrobe. All her life, my mother's appearance had been very important to her. Even after being confined to her wheelchair at home, she exerted the effort everyday to dress in a well-appointed outfit that typically included a skirt, a top, a jacket of some sort and either jewelry or a scarf. My mother always appeared as if she were ready to go to church. This routine continued in her new community. She actually had enough clothes in her inventory to wear a different outfit daily for at least a month, all seasons of the year. This was thanks in part to my sister, Marilee, who loved to go to high quality consignment and upscale thrift stores in her Florida community, and who was constantly sending my mom apparel. And my mom, herself, never missed a Friday at the on-site thrift shop where she frequently found treasures to add to her wardrobe or pass on to one of us.

* * *

One evening in February, a couple of months after she sent out the Christmas epistle, I received a phone call from her nurse saying that my mom was being transported by ambulance to a Richmond hospital. Still capable of speaking for herself, mom apparently had done her best to resist leaving the facility for medical care. However, the nursing staff, as my mother explained to me later, patiently persuaded my mom that they did not possess the resources to address medical needs relating to her heart. Ultimately she acceded to their recommendation and granted them permission to be transported to the same hospital that had been the provider for her hospice care before she was discharged.

My husband and I arrived at the Emergency Department soon after the ambulance brought her, to quite a drama. Apparently the Emergency Department was so busy that night that my mother's ambulance was the last one to admit a patient before the hospital began diverting incoming potential patents to other local hospitals. The waiting room of the Emergency Department seemed like a scene from a homeless shelter or refugee camp, with people all over the place, including sitting on the floor, waiting; however, though the area was crowded, it was not chaotic in any way.

We were immediately ushered into the cubicle where my mom was holding court with an EMT apprentice and his supervisor. Apparently the situation was *all hands on deck* so the ambulance staff was assisting the Emergency Department personnel. Additionally, there was an aid, from the facility, sitting with my mother. Mom appeared to be doing quite well; she didn't seem in distress at all; presumably the interventions initiated in the ambulance had begun to take effect.

My husband and I stayed a while, called family members and eventually were informed that as soon as a room became available, which might be a long wait, my mother would officially be admitted. Because it was already after midnight - and knowing my husband and I had to work that day - my mother insisted we leave, assuring us she would be fine. Judging from the attentiveness of the staff it was clear our presence wasn't needed so we heeded her advice; promising to return later that day. By this time we had been informed that mom's hospital stay was expected to be a minimum of several days.

We learned the next day that because of the random availability of beds, my mother had been given a private room in a special women's unit; an upgrade from what is a typical hospital room. Mom quickly became fond of her caregivers, befriended the other staff and embraced the benefits of being waited on. She actually was not experiencing much pain or discomfort. A cardiologist was monitoring her heart to determine the most effective protocol and medication to prescribe.

Annilee and Susan came for an extended visit so mom would have advocates during her hospitalization. However, their presence wasn't really required because the staff was extremely attentive and caring, my mom had no problem advocating for herself, and the hospital stay overall was reassuringly upbeat.

Before mom's return to her community was scheduled, a physician met with her (while my two sisters were present) to give the details of the discharge plan. The physician explained to my mother that he was increasing the dosage of her diuretic, a medication that causes an increase in urine output. My mother had always been a minimalist when it came to the need for any medication; she was happiest taking none or as little as possible, so for her this was not good news.

The doctor's prescription change increasing her diuretic distressed her greatly and she challenged him. According to my sisters' account, this amazed the physician; apparently he was not accustomed to having his orders questioned. However, to his credit he listened to my mother's objections. She gave a passionate, eloquent plea stating that if she abided by his new orders it would greatly erode her quality of life. She listed the activities she routinely engaged in and explained how she moved to a variety of venues on the campus for pottery, fitness activities, book and poetry clubs, chapel services and special events. Then she described how every time she had to go to the bathroom, she would have to return to her room in the convalescent center to have a staff member assist her, and many of the venues she visited were a considerable distance from her room. Thus, there was no way she'd be able to continue participating in these activities and this medication change would in essence greatly diminish her quality of life.

Allegedly, the doctor was somewhat taken aback by her earnest fervor. My guess is this doctor had not encountered too many ninety-one-year old women with hundred percent scores on mini-mental tests, an unquenchable zest for life and such convincing oratory skills.

To the doctor's credit he let my Mom have her say, truly listening to her wishes. Then he explained that he could adjust the timing of the medication and he also could lower the dosage, but she needed to know that doing so could decrease her life expectancy; it could very well cause her to die sooner than she would by not choosing to adhere to his recommendation. My mom then countered that if she didn't have the wherewithal to maintain the full life she was leading, there would be little point to extending her life. If she took the increased medication, her life would be like circling in a plane while waiting for the landing, instead of getting on with the journey. So, the physician lowered the diuretic dosage so Mom could live as fully as she had been.

Mom returned to her community, not worse for wear. She resumed her busy schedule. She also, for some unknown reason, decided that she wanted to be put back under Hospice Services. Perhaps she looked at doing this as a means of preventing another hospitalization, or possibly she, at some level had a presentiment of what the future held.

The convalescent center nursing staff conveyed her request to Hospice, and immediately the primary nurse who had been assigned to Mom a year and a half earlier paid her a visit. She researched my mom's chart to evaluate appropriateness for Hospice services. The nurse took the medical information back to the Hospice team and initially mom's readmission was refused; Hospice staff could not come up with medical documentation, which indicated my mother was Hospice appropriate. The thoughtful and competent Hospice nurse really wanted to be able to admit my mom but Medicare has specific guidelines for admission. A case has to be made that an individual is not expected, with their medical disease and condition, to live more than six months.

My husband and I made a Saturday visit to my mom after she got the "bittersweet" news that she wasn't sick enough to become a Hospice patient. We had a good visit and other than her disappointment from that news, everything was as it had been. Before we left, Mother General asked me to do several things for her: order two books online and purchase a new battery for her watch.

As my husband and I were saying our goodbyes that Saturday afternoon, my mother had some parting words for my husband - something to the effect - *I'm so happy you and Janna found each other. You've been a wonderful husband and son-in-law.*

As we walked to the parking lot I remarked to my husband, with some element of wonder, that my mother's comments sounded like *end of life talk.* He agreed.

The next day, Sunday, I received a phone call from the nurse from Hospice who'd been advocating for mom's readmission. Apparently, the nurse had met with the Hospice medical director, who had an office in the hospital where Mom had had her recent stay. The doctor was able to do further research utilizing mom's recent hospital records regarding her medical condition and the Hospice physician was able to come up with documentation that would allow her to be readmitted to Hospice. With Hospice policy to contact family members, the nurse was calling to let me know the decision and that she and my mother would be filling out the admission paperwork Monday, which was the next day.

Very early Tuesday morning I was awoken by a phone call from the nurse manager at my mother's facility informing me that my mother was not doing well. I was totally taken aback. Two days earlier my mom had been fine. As a chaplain, I was aware that 4:00 a.m. phone calls are not made casually and medical professionals frequently use words or phrases like, "not doing well" or "serious," to soften the reality that someone has taken a major turn for the worse. To confirm what she was attempting to convey to me, I responded, *"Are you telling me that my mother is actively dying?"* The nurse responded that she couldn't say that but that things looked very serious.

I immediately dressed, notified my workplace of the situation, drove to Richmond and went directly to my mother's room in the convalescent center. I found my mother unresponsive; she was either sleeping heavily or in a coma. A nurse came in and described how the previous evening my mother was put to bed and at the time everything seemed normal. Mom had set her hair in rollers, taken her medication and gone to bed.

However, before too long she began experiencing some breathing issues, and she coughed up some blood. My mother and the nurse conversed about hospitalization but my mother, being under Hospice care as of that morning, was adamant she not be sent to the hospital, and instead requested a call be made to the Hospice on-call nurse. The call was made and my mother was prescribed some additional medication that quickly alleviated her discomfort, and enabled her to sleep. When the staff made their rounds early the next morning, her condition was deemed unresponsive - she was breathing but couldn't be aroused - and so at that point the staff nurse called Hospice again and she also notified me.

It's strange the memories one retains from those moments in life that are fraught with significance. I remember that, for a day in early March, it was extremely warm and I found it necessary to open the window. I remember the clothes I was wearing, snippets of conversations held and kindnesses rendered. On the other hand, the actual sequence of events is somewhat blurred.

* * *

I do recall that after arriving, I conversed with the nurse; and when it registered that my mother might be actively dying, I began calling the sisters who could be reached. It was difficult to know what to tell them. My mother was believed to be dying, and probably would not regain consciousness, but one could not be sure. And, as my sisters and I realized from the experience with my dad, people can be in an actively dying state for as few as hours to a number of days.

Several of my sisters were scheduled to visit in the coming two weeks. Because Linnea was in the middle of the Atlantic Ocean, on the home stretch of her three-month world cruise, I felt there was no purpose in notifying her at this point of what was transpiring. Marilee, living in Florida, had airline tickets to visit around the time of Linnea's return so, though I let her know what appeared to be going on; she decided to wait and see what occurred before she changed her plans. Annilee - scheduled momentarily to board a plane in Maryland for a vacation in California that she and her husband had been eagerly anticipating - had only minutes to agonize about whether to go with her husband or come to Richmond. She chose, hesitantly, to follow through on her plans. Despite the fact she was suffering from a respiratory illness, Donna, in New York, offered to make the eleven-hour trip, but we both felt that wasn't the best plan. Carol was house sitting for a friend in New Zealand, so she too was unavailable. Susan, in the D.C. area that day, was representing the think-tank she worked for as a co-convener of an important daylong conference. However, she said the significant responsibilities that were hers had already been carried out and her co-convener could handle the rest of the conference without her. She realized that though her body might remain present at the conference, if she chose not to come, her mind and soul would be otherwise engaged. Thus, she handed over her professional responsibilities, and quickly packed some clothes to come share the vigil with me. I was reminded of the quip one of my sisters made during my dad's illness, *"Seven is not enough!"*

The wonderful Hospice chaplain, who my mom loved, came by and in his presence I realized the rollers in my mom's hair did not accord her much dignity. So, I removed them and attempted to style her hair. For my mother, appearance was very important and, especially on her deathbed, I needed to honor this value she held. And it's a good thing I did.

It's always been fascinating to me how word magically gets around a facility when a resident's condition has changed, so as I expected - despite health care's confidentiality code - a sequence of visitors began appearing at my mother's door. A parade of aids, nurses, and housekeepers, plus friends and other staff came by to bid my mother goodbye.

Fortunately, before too many visitors had found their way to my mother's room, my sister arrived. Though my mother's condition was unchanged, visitors would talk to her and wish her well. Some expressed their gratitude to her for being supportive, caring, a good friend, an inspiration, and confidant during the two years they had known her. Others shared stories with us about experiences they'd had together. My sister and I were profoundly touched by the sincerity expressed and the number of visitors who made their way to our door. The facility staff was extremely thoughtful, bringing us trays of food, offering assistance, and just letting us know they were there for us.

* * *

As our ancestors predominately did, most Americans want to die at home, but only about twenty-five percent do. Around forty percent of deaths occur in a hospital or institution. In the sixteen years at the Retirement Community where I served, I'd witnessed and been part of a gradual promising evolution about the approach to death and how to care for the actively dying; both in our facility and in the community. More individuals were utilizing Hospice services and so fewer seriously ill residents were sent to the Emergency Room for aggressive treatment that often just prolonged the dying process. The Williamsburg Community had constructed a beautiful four bed Hospice House where not only the terminally ill "guests" were served, but where family members also were ministered to. Facilities, such as the one I worked in and the one my mother resided in, tried to emulate similar dying-at-home type of experiences. With or without the cooperation of the Hospice team, our staff delivered comfort, and offered sensitive and dignified care for those who were close to their lives' end. For many, the facility was their home; our residents, and my mother were, in essence, having a dying at home experience.

* * *

Morning became afternoon and soon evening arrived. Things quieted down with the visitors and Susan had the inspiration to read to my mother. Though my mother was not alert, oriented, or able to speak or respond, she was probably aware of our presence on some level and could possibly hear. I had always been told and believed that the last senses to go are hearing and touch. Susan thought it'd be nice to read to Mom from the autobiographical memoir she, herself, had authored, *"Serendipitously I Roll."*

So, totally unaware of the power of what we were about to read, at the bedside of my dying mother, my sister and I began taking turns reading aloud from her book's beginning. Fittingly, in the first chapter, my mother wrote about her dad, our grandfather.

We read along and then got to this portion of my mother's memories regarding her father:

In his later years, my father suffered from angina, but this did not keep him from doing things. He just did things more slowly. One day he was in great pain, and I thought I was going to lose him. I started to cry. In the midst of his pain he followed his own advice; he did not indulge in self-pity. Ever the optimist, he said, "Bernice, don't feel sad if I die. I'll be better off. Always remember that." That made it easier for me to let him go when the time came. He lived life to the hilt, but he was able to accept the end of life with grace and dignity.........

Talk about messages from the universe! Here we were, present at my dying mother's bedside, hearing a message she had taken to heart near the time of her father's death, which undoubtedly would be the message she'd want to convey at that particular moment to all her offspring. *"Girls, don't feel sad if I die. I'll be better off. Always remember that."*

These words from my mother's book brought back memories surrounding my grandfather's death, the first of my four grandparents to die. I was newly married and living in Texas, where my husband was a graduate student, when we received word that Grandpa had died. Though my grandfather had coped with heart ailments for a long time, his death was still devastating to me. For four years, while I attended college, I lived in the town where he resided and we became very close. While I was a student, because of issues with dizziness he had wisely relinquished his driving privileges, so I often chauffeured him around town. I also worked part-time, in one of the paint stores he opened many years previously, and frequently shared meals with him and my grandmother.

Grandpa's life was an American success story. By himself, he had emigrated from Sweden when he was a teenager. He and my grandmother, a Scandinavian immigrant, worked hard and had a thriving paint business that included six retail stores and a paint factory that my uncles were running. Grandpa had always been larger than life and someone I greatly admired and loved.

Upon arriving in his town - the town my mother grew up in - for the funeral, I realized that I had forgotten my birth control pills. I shared this information with my mother, (who had informed me as part of my pre-wedding advice to use the pill because it was the only birth control method that worked) and she hurriedly made an appointment for me with my grandfather's physician, who had been her family's long time doctor.

I was successful getting the birth control prescription, but the unforgettable part of the encounter was the doctor telling me that my grandfather had *given up* and that's why he died. These words, *"Your grandfather died because he gave up,"* devastated me but I resolved, because I didn't want anyone else to feel the impact of his words, not to share this information at that time.

It was years later, after my experiences as a Hospice Chaplain, that I was able to reframe those insensitive words spoken by that family doctor. Because my grandmother could no longer care for my grandfather, he had been moved to a nursing facility. He was extremely weak, and his major pastime was sleeping. He was totally dependent on others for his care. His disease was progressive, he suffered a lot of pain and there was no hope for recovery. Ultimately, the time came when the fitting response, and possibly the only response, was to let go, to let nature take its course and allow death to come. That, I now understand, is definitely not giving up. This doctor, who apparently viewed death as losing a medical battle, or as stopping a relentless search for longevity, had not learned the difference between giving up and letting go.

At my dying mother's bedside, this reflection gave me comfort because it was clear to me that my mother was letting go, letting nature take its course. At some level, she accepted that we were not created to live forever and there really is a time to be born and a time to die, and the time was upon us.

* * *

My sister and I, deciding to maintain our vigil, were supplied with a mattress and we tried to get some sleep. Lying on the floor we could hear my mother's breathing. The night nurses promised to check her periodically to see if she needed additional medication or any other care. However, the scenario of my mother dying while we were sleeping was not appealing to me and prevented me from falling asleep. I remember laying there hearing, in the distance, the howling of a night train and how its keening sound matched my spirit.

Before too long I could hear my mother's breathing pattern change and so I decided to sit up with her. Changes in an actively dying person's breathing can be an indication that death is imminent. Often a final breathing pattern is when the mouth of a person, not actually taking in much air, gasps or puffs. That is what appeared to be happening. So, at some level, I wasn't too shocked when, after a time, her breathing changed and ended; she peacefully let go. Feeling numb, I woke Susan up and told her Mom had died. We shared some quiet time talking, telling stories, laughing about funny memories, trying to acknowledge the reality that our mother was dead and we were orphans. In time, I alerted the nurse.

Celebrating a Life Well Ended

Amazingly it was less than a day from the time my mother became unconscious, until she died. From being her normal self, to becoming unresponsive, to dying, for my mother had been a quick journey. In contemplating this I realized that such was her mode of handling life's demands. Once she planned something, she set to doing her part to make it happen as quickly as possible; by taking care of all that was needed. It seems that this is how she handled her last earthly act – at some level knowing it was time, she finalized her burial arrangements, set Hospice in place, issued indirect farewell messages, and then got on with the deed.

I can't help but believe that after bearing witness to all that my father had endured, my mother was extra motivated to do all she was capable of to have a smooth, quick, peaceful ending. Before the quality of her life deteriorated, to a point she did not consider to be acceptable, she let go. She had done what she could to engineer a swift dying time.

* * *

Though it was late and we were - needless to say - exhausted, my sister and I drove an hour to my home in Williamsburg where we got cleaned up and attempted to get some sleep before we returned early the next morning to begin the task of sorting through my mother's belongings.

It had been an incredibly long day. The only way I could describe how I felt, other than exhausted, was like a Raggedy Ann doll that had lost its stuffing. I had nothing left in me at all.

We returned the next morning to clean out my mother's room. A staff member came by and invited us to a complimentary lunch in the independent dining room where my mom had regularly dined. We arrived at a table where several of her friends sat. On the table in the center of the place setting, where my mother typically ate, lay a long-stemmed red rose. My sister and I were overcome with tears, and as the waitress approached, Susan asked, *"Do you do this for everyone who dies?"* Looking gently into my sister's eyes, the waitress answered, *"No, this is the first time."* That was one of many thoughtful acts we experienced from those who had cared for her at her adopted Virginia home.

The day we were setting up the reception for my mother's service, one of the staff stopped by bearing a piece of pottery. It was a very attractive serving plate with hand-painted designs on it. The coordinator who brought it said she thought we might like to have this plate because it was the last piece of pottery my mother had crafted in her class.

Several weeks after my mom's death, my sister and I received a note from her retirement community's chief executive officer that included the words, *"Let it be clear. Your mother gave more to this place than we provided to her."* Something tells me that was a sentiment that few residents' family members received. All of these meaningful gestures made our loss a little more bearable.

It was evident that a lot of my mother's new friends were mourning her passing and since two of my sisters from afar had already scheduled trips to Richmond, we decided to hold a memorial service at my mother's community.

Assembling the extended family together would take more planning than a few days or weeks, so my sisters and I decided to have this first memorial service at my mother's retirement community and then plan an interment of her ashes in the summer at the grave in New York where my dad was buried for our extended family and any friends.

Working with the wonderful chaplains at her facility, we planned a memorial service. Over two hundred people attended. Amazingly, my mother, though a resident of the convalescent center, had cultivated friendships throughout the entire facility both with those who lived there and those who worked there.

Prior to the service, as my sister and I were sorting through my mother's belongings, I came across two plastic bags filled with carefully pressed cloth handkerchiefs. There were delicately embroidered and colorful, and each one was unique. The bags contained well over a hundred hankies. I held up the bags and asked my sister if she knew anything about them. Susan replied that my mother had been saving them to be given as favors on the occasion of her funeral. Leave it to my mother. She loved to give little gifts to people when they visited her or on special or social occasions, and apparently because she considered her final farewell such an occasion, she made provisions to enact this ritual.

* * *

In her final years my mother had been an example to all of us in how to embrace the changes life brings, how to soldier on seeking new experiences, and how to live creatively the life one was given. In her concluding days she had shown us how to die well: by assessing what makes a quality life, assertively insisting on it, and when that is no longer plausible, letting it go peacefully. Having felt the pain and anguish of my father's final months, she had learned that one's choices impact one's endings. And her choice was to not prolong her dying but to allow nature to take its course.

Postlude

This story, chronicling my parents dying times, uncovers the strikingly different endings of my father's and mother's lives; deaths separated not only by time - eight years - but also by a myriad of decisions and circumstances - inspiring, anguishing, humorous, and heartbreaking. If there is anything we, family members and friends, learned by companioning my parents through their ending times, it is that as often as not, individuals have options in shaping their final days. And for most individuals, a major determining factor seems to be the amount of healthcare and intervention a person is willing to accept or decline. My father's experience taught us that though medical professionals prescribe or recommend a procedure, therapy or treatment (with good intentions), undertaking that recommendation might not be in the best interests of the patient.

Furthermore, it needs to be said when a person does give their assent to treat, the decision is revocable. Though often difficult to actually carry out, and something patients don't often realize they are entitled to even suggest, is discontinuing or withholding a previously agreed-upon intervention. However, this is not the usual action because no one, neither the patient nor a medical professional, acknowledge that the patient is dying and intervention is not going to actually save the life, it will only prolong the dying, and often the suffering. The question shouldn't be, *"Will I continue fighting to stay alive?"* but more significantly, *"What will life be like if I do continue the struggle? Will it include the elements of living that I consider worthwhile?"*

In order to answer those questions, each person must decide individually what constitutes a life of quality, what those elements of living would be. For some it might be to enjoy food; for others, to recognize and find pleasure in the presence of friends and family; for some, to be able to be physically independent.

In retrospect it's apparent that my father was communicating that his life, as he was living it, did not have the quality to make it worthwhile. On a number of occasions he expressed that coherently: when he told Linnea he *"can't go on like this,"* in his first week at the nursing facility when he asked, *"did Mr. M stopped eating because he couldn't take it anymore,"* after several weeks in the rehab he referred to himself as, *"a prisoner being tortured every day,"* the occasion when he waxed eloquently about how he wished he were, in his *"favorite restaurant, or cooking his morning egg in his own kitchen"*, or when he said that he'd follow the doctor's advice and have the feeding tube reinserted because he couldn't, *"promise to eat enough orally"* (like he was even capable of that), or when he asked for statistics halfway through his rehab on, *"success of the kind of operation"* he'd had, or when he mentioned *hospice* to his surgeon, or when he eventually asked about getting rid of the feeding tube.

However, throughout the entire ordeal the push was for fighting to live, in other words, life at any cost. Sadly no one, including myself, offered my father the opportunity to clarify which factors he required to make his life worth fighting for. Though we will never know if we had done so if it would have mitigated his suffering and enhanced the time he did live, we have all learned there are alternatives to doing all that can be done, and downsides to taking advantage of treatments just because they are available.

My mother's experience taught us that we are entitled to our own opinion of what a life with quality looks like. For her it meant being free to convey herself around her facility. If medical protocol threatened that freedom, she did not want to follow it. And though she possibly did shorten her life by choosing to take a lower dose of medicine, she lived a life of quality according to her standards to the last day.

It might seem strange coming from a clergy person, but sadly part of what has caused this perspective, choosing life at all costs, to be dominant, has been religious views. Some denominational doctrines and religious mandates have held their believers hostage to having to choose life at all costs. Not doing so for them has been defined as suicide. Such a perspective may have been appropriate at one time.

However, in our current medical environment when machines, medicine and treatments can prolong life indefinitely, this is no longer the case. I believe it is more reverential to ascertain if a life with meaning is possible, than to keep a heart beating in a body just because we have the capability to do so.

Amid traumatic situations, perspective often is skewed or clouded and decision-making is based on wishful thinking, fear, hope, misunderstanding or an array of other things. Though it's not a pleasant endeavor, preparing for the time when one will be facing life and death choices is imperative. By documenting desired treatment, informing loved ones of what constitutes quality of life, and openly communicating desires and wishes for a time when you might be unable to speak for yourself, you will make the ending season of life less traumatic and more peaceful. Preparation also can prove to be a great source of guidance and consolation to your loved ones as they make this journey with you, because you are gifting them with the confidence that your wishes are being honored.

Though my parents conceivably had no idea they were still conveying life lessons, I will always be grateful for what I learned from them and their experiences, to their dying days, when visiting hours ended.

ABOUT THE AUTHOR

Janna Roche is a semi-retired chaplain. Before moving to Williamsburg in 1998, she was Chaplain at Hamilton College in Clinton, New York and spiritual care coordinator at the Utica Hospice. Since she's been in Williamsburg, she's served as chaplain at the Hospice House and spent sixteen years as chaplain at Patriots Colony Retirement Community. Currently Janna works part time at Bucktrout Funeral Home, the oldest continuously operating funeral home in the United States.

A